It's another star from the CGP galaxy...

Here's the thing: you can't cut corners when it comes to Grade 9-1 GCSE Physics.
You really have to practise until you're 100% confident about every topic.

That's where this indispensable CGP book comes in. It's bursting with questions just
like the ones you'll face in the real exams, including those tricky required practicals.

And since you'll be tested on a wide range of topics in the real exams,
we've also included a section of mixed questions to keep you on your toes!

CGP — still the best! ☺

Our sole aim here at CGP is to produce the highest quality books —
carefully written, immaculately presented and dangerously close to being funny.

Then we work our socks off to get them out to you
— at the cheapest possible prices.

Contents

✓ Use the tick boxes to check off the topics you've completed.

Published by CGP.

Editors:
Emily Garrett, Sharon Keeley-Holden, Duncan Lindsay, Frances Rooney, Sarah Williams

Contributors:
Mark A. Edwards

With thanks to Lucy Johnson and Karen Wells for the proofreading.
With thanks to Ana Pungartnik for the copyright research.

ISBN: 978 1 78294 507 9

Graph to show trend in Atmospheric CO_2 Concentration and global temperature on page 13
based on data by EPICA community members 2004 and Siegenthaler et al 2005.

Clipart from Corel®
Printed by Elanders Ltd, Newcastle upon Tyne.

Based on the classic CGP style created by Richard Parsons.

How to Use This Book

- Hold the book <u>upright</u>, approximately <u>50 cm</u> from your face, ensuring that the text looks like <u>this</u>, not ~~sıɥʇ~~. Alternatively, place the book on a <u>horizontal</u> surface (e.g. a table or desk) and sit adjacent to the book, at a distance which doesn't make the text too small to read.

- In case of emergency, press the two halves of the book together <u>firmly</u> in order to close.

- Before attempting to use this book, familiarise yourself with the following <u>safety information</u>:

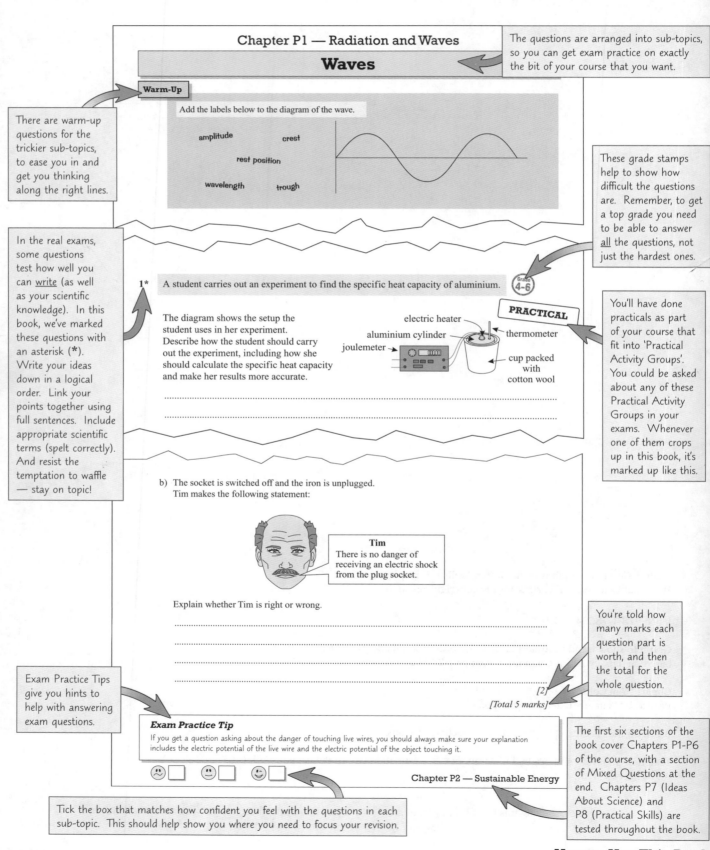

The questions are arranged into sub-topics, so you can get exam practice on exactly the bit of your course that you want.

There are warm-up questions for the trickier sub-topics, to ease you in and get you thinking along the right lines.

These grade stamps help to show how difficult the questions are. Remember, to get a top grade you need to be able to answer <u>all</u> the questions, not just the hardest ones.

In the real exams, some questions test how well you can <u>write</u> (as well as your scientific knowledge). In this book, we've marked these questions with an asterisk (*). Write your ideas down in a logical order. Link your points together using full sentences. Include appropriate scientific terms (spelt correctly). And resist the temptation to waffle — stay on topic!

You'll have done practicals as part of your course that fit into 'Practical Activity Groups'. You could be asked about any of these Practical Activity Groups in your exams. Whenever one of them crops up in this book, it's marked up like this.

You're told how many marks each question part is worth, and then the total for the whole question.

Exam Practice Tips give you hints to help with answering exam questions.

The first six sections of the book cover Chapters P1-P6 of the course, with a section of Mixed Questions at the end. Chapters P7 (Ideas About Science) and P8 (Practical Skills) are tested throughout the book.

Tick the box that matches how confident you feel with the questions in each sub-topic. This should help show you where you need to focus your revision.

Waves

Add the labels below to the diagram of the wave.

amplitude   crest

rest position

wavelength   trough

1 Which of the following is **not** a transverse wave?
Place a tick (✓) in the box next to the correct answer.

Grade 4-6

waves on a rope □

light waves □

sound waves in air ✓

ripples in water □

[Total 1 mark]

2 Waves can be either transverse or longitudinal.   *Grade 4-6*

Describe the difference between longitudinal and transverse waves.

Longitudinal waves are parallel to the direction

it travels, Transverse waves are perpendicular

[Total 2 marks]

3 A signal generator is used to produce a wave on a spring, as shown in the diagram below.   *Grade 4-6*

X

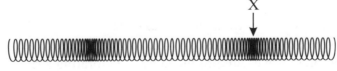

a) Label a compression and a rarefaction on the diagram above.

[2]

b) The signal generator is turned on for 50 s. During this time, 400 complete cycles of the wave pass point X. Calculate the frequency of the wave.

$$\frac{400}{50}$$

Frequency = ...8.......... Hz

[2]

[Total 4 marks]

4 A child throws a stone into a pond. The stone creates ripples when it hits the water, which spread across the pond.

a) The ripples pass a leaf floating on the pond.
State whether or not the leaf will be carried to the edge of the pond. Explain your answer.

......Waves....transfer.....energy..,so..the..ripples..don't.......

....move..water..or....the....leaf....from..one...place...to.......

....another..

[2]

b) The ripples have a wavelength of 15 mm. Given that their frequency is 1.4×10^{-2} kHz, calculate their speed in m/s. Show your working.

$\frac{15}{1000} = 0.015m$

$1.4 \times 10^{-3} \times 1000 = 14 Hz$

14×0.015
$= 0.21 m/s$

Speed = ...0.21.......... m/s

[4]

[Total 6 marks]

5 A vibrating violin string produces a sound wave. A violinist is practising in a village hall. Her teacher sits at the back of the hall to listen.

a) State the medium the sound waves travel through to reach the teacher.

......Air...

[1]

b) The violinist plays a note with a frequency of 2.49 kHz. The sound waves travel at a speed of 340 m/s. Calculate the wavelength of the sound waves.
Give your answer to **two** significant figures.

2.49×1000 $\frac{340}{2496} = 0.136$
$= 2490$

Wavelength = ..0.14............... m

[4]

c) The violinist then plays a note with a frequency of 220 Hz.
The violinist plays this note for 5.0 seconds.
Calculate how many complete waves are produced by the vibrating string in this time.

220×5

$= 1100$

Number of waves = ...1100........

[2]

[Total 7 marks]

Exam Practice Tip
You'll often be given a frequency in kHz, which stands for kilohertz. Don't let this put you off — just remember to convert it to Hz before using it in an equation. To convert it, you need to know that 1000 Hz = 1 kHz.

Wave Experiments

1   Aria is investigating water waves in a ripple tank. She sets up the equipment shown below.

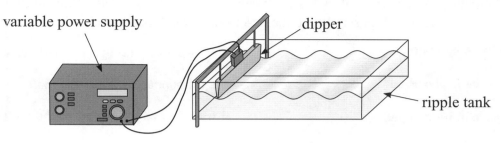

a) Aria wants to measure the frequency of the ripples. She floats a cork in the ripple tank and measures the time it takes for the cork to oscillate 30 times. Aria repeats her experiment five times. She does not adjust the variable power supply between repeats.

State **two** other factors that should remain the same between repeats.

....

....
[2]

b) The table below shows Aria's results. She recorded one of the results incorrectly.

Trial	1	2	3	4	5
Time taken for 30 oscillations (seconds)	36	33	63	33	42

Calculate the average time taken for the cork to oscillate 30 times, ignoring the anomalous result.

Time for 30 oscillations = ... s
[2]

c) Using your answer to **part b)**, calculate the frequency of the ripples. Give your answer to **two** significant figures.

Frequency = ... Hz
[3]

d) Aria's friend Cass suggests they could use the ripple tank to measure the speed of the ripples. Describe a method they could use.

....

....

....

....

....

....
[3]

[Total 10 marks]

Reflection and Refraction

At the boundary with a new material, a wave can be reflected, absorbed or transmitted.
Draw a line to match each possibility to the description which best matches it.

wave is reflected — it passes through the material

wave is absorbed — it bounces back off the material

wave is transmitted — it transfers all its energy to the material

1   When a wave passes through a boundary between materials, it can change direction.   (Grade 4-6)

a) Name this effect.

...Refraction... ✓

[1]

b) A light ray hits a glass block and passes through it without changing direction.
Give the angle to the surface at which the light ray hit the glass block.

Angle to the surface = ...90...... °

[1]

[Total 2 marks]

2   Luke is investigating the refraction of light waves. He models this using water waves
in a tank with sections of different depths. The figure below is a wavefront diagram
showing the path of a water wave as it travels from Section 1 to Section 2 of the tank.   (Grade 6-7)

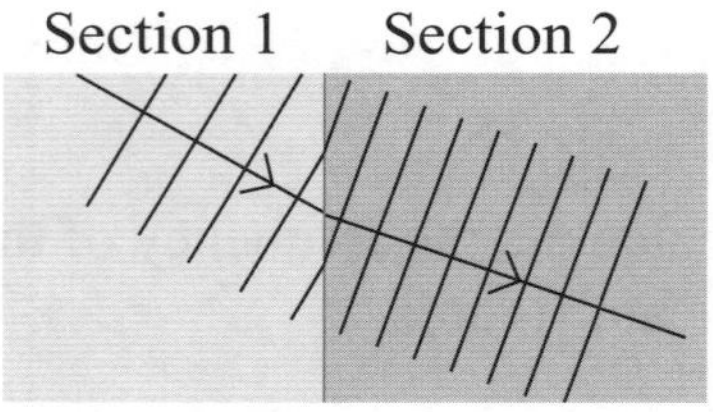

Section 1   Section 2

a) When a water wave travels into shallower water it slows down.
State **one** conclusion you can make about the depth of the water in Section 2,
compared to that in Section 1.

...The wave refracts (bends) Section 2 is
shallower than Section 1.

[1]

b) Light waves travel at different speeds in different materials, so the different water depths in the
tank represent the different materials. Describe how the frequency and wavelength of the water
wave changes as it enters Section 2.

...As the water wave enters Section 2, the
frequency of the wave remains the
same .

[2]

[Total 3 marks]

Reflection and Refraction Experiments

PRACTICAL

1   Tamika is investigating refraction through different materials. She uses a laser to shine a ray of light into prisms made of different materials (but identical in size and shape), at a fixed angle, I. She traces the path of the ray entering and leaving the prism on a sheet of paper.

Once she has traced the rays, Tamika traces around the edge of the prism, and removes the prism. She draws normals to the surface at the points the ray entered and exited the prism.

The diagram below shows Tamika's investigation for light refracted through a glass prism.

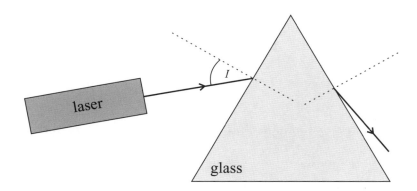

a) Complete the diagram above by drawing in the refracted ray through the prism.
    Mark the angle of refraction, R, of the light ray as it enters the prism.

[1]

The table below shows the results for prisms of different materials.

Material	I	R
Cubic zirconia	40°	17°
Sapphire	40°	22°
Plastic	40°	27°

b) State which of the materials shown in the table above changes the speed of the light ray the least.
    Explain your answer.

....

....

....

[3]

c) Suggest a suitable graph or chart Tamika could use to present her data.
    Give **one** reason for your answer.

....

....

[2]

[Total 6 marks]

2 Scott wants to investigate the relationship between the angle of incidence
and the angle of reflection when light is reflected by a mirror.
He has a mirror, a ray box, a large sheet of paper and a protractor.

a) Describe how Scott could carry out his investigation.
Include a labelled diagram showing the angles he should measure.

....

....

....

....

....

[6]

b) Explain why Scott used a ray box as the light source in this experiment.

....

....

[2]

The table below shows Scott's results.

Angle of incidence / °	15	30	45	60	75
Angle of reflection / °	18	33	48	63	78

c) State what kind of error these results show. Suggest what may have caused it.

....

....

[2]

[Total 10 marks]

Exam Practice Tip

Remember, when you're dealing with angles of incidence and refraction, they're measured from the normal to the ray,
not from the surface. Make sure you have a sharp pencil and a ruler for drawing rays and marking angles in the exam.

Chapter P1 — Radiation and Waves

The Electromagnetic Spectrum

Warm-Up

For each sentence, circle whether it is true or false.

All electromagnetic waves are longitudinal.   **True** / **False**

All electromagnetic waves travel at the same speed in space (a vacuum).   **True** / **False**

Gamma rays can be emitted from the nucleus of an atom.   **True** / **False**

1   Sonya is discussing the electromagnetic spectrum.

Sonya
The electromagnetic spectrum covers a range of frequencies, human eyes can detect a large part of it.

Explain which part of Sonya's statement is incorrect.

Eyes cannot detect a large part of it. It can only detect visible light.

[Total 1 mark]

2   Spacesuits worn by astronauts are designed to protect them from ionising UV radiation. The intensity of UV radiation from the Sun that reaches the Earth and the Moon is roughly the same, but the Moon has no atmosphere.   (Grade 7-9)

Describe how humans are protected from ionising UV radiation on Earth. Explain why this does not occur on the Moon.

a There is a layer called the ozone layer. The ozone layer absorbs any UV radiation which then protects us.

[Total 4 marks]

                      Chapter P1 — Radiation and Waves

Energy Levels and Ionisation

Use the words in the box to correctly fill in the gaps in the passage.
You don't have to use every word, but each word can only be used once.

The electrons around an atom are at .... distances

from the nucleus. An electron moves .... the

nucleus when it absorbs EM radiation.

> closer to
>
> further from
>
> different
>
> identical

1   Some types of electromagnetic wave can be harmful to people.   Grade 4-6

a) Ultraviolet radiation can be harmful to humans, as it can ionise atoms or molecules in our cells.
State what is meant when an atom is said to have been 'ionised'.

    They have a charge An electron
    has been removed.

    [1]

b) Give **two** damaging effects of ultraviolet radiation.

    1. Mutation of cells

    2. Cancer

    [2]

c) Other than ultraviolet radiation, name **one** type of electromagnetic radiation which is ionising.

    Infrared X-rays

    [1]

    [Total 4 marks]

2   A fluorescent tube light contains mercury vapour and has a coating of
phosphorus on the inside. When the light is on, electrons in the atoms of
the mercury are excited, which leads to UV radiation being emitted. This
radiation is absorbed by the phosphorus atoms, which then emit visible light.   Grade 7-9

a) Describe the changes within the mercury atoms that leads to UV radiation being released.

    Excited electrons fell back down to
    their original energy level.

    [2]

b) Explain why mercury and phosphorus atoms emit different forms of electromagnetic radiation.

    The part of the EM spectrum what
    the radiation is from depend on
    the frequency of the radiation.

    [3]

    [Total 5 marks]

Uses of EM Radiation

1 Microwaves are a type of electromagnetic radiation with many useful applications. (Grade 4-6)

a) Which of the following is a use of microwave radiation?
Place a tick (✓) in the box next to the correct answer.

artificial suntanning ☐

cancer treatment ☐

satellite communications ☑

medical imaging ☐

[1]

b) Suggest **one** other use of microwave radiation.

Cooking food ✓

[1]

[Total 2 marks]

2 Gamma radiation can be used to sterilise medical instruments, such as syringes and needles. (Grade 6-7)

Suggest **two** reasons why gamma rays are used to sterilise these items.

They kill bacteria that we cannot see to prevent infections.

[Total 2 marks]

3 Colin thinks he has broken his arm. His doctor sends him to the hospital to have an X-ray image made of his arm. (Grade 6-7)

X-ray images are formed using an X-ray source and a photographic plate.
The part of the body being imaged is placed between the X-ray source and the plate.

The plate initially appears white. When part of the plate is hit by X-ray radiation, it absorbs the radiation and turns black.

a) Suggest how X-rays form an image on the plate of the bones in Colin's arm.
You should refer to the absorption and transmission of the X-rays in your answer.

The X-rays are emitted to to his arm which absorbs it and is transmitted.

[3]

b) Colin notices that the staff who work with the X-ray machines wear badges that monitor the levels of radiation they have been exposed to.

Explain why it is important to make sure hospital staff are exposed to as little X-ray radiation as possible.

So they don't get affected by radiation as it could harm them.

[1]

[Total 4 marks]

4* Mako is using a walkie-talkie to communicate with another worker on a construction site. Walkie-talkies transmit radio waves between each other. When Mako speaks into the microphone, it creates an electric current. When the other worker's walkie-talkie receives a message, its microphone becomes a loudspeaker and converts electrical current into sound waves.

Grade 7-9

Briefly describe the steps involved for the creation, transmission and reception of a radio wave between a pair of walkie-talkies. You do not need to describe how microphones or loudspeakers work.

Walkie-talkies transmit radio waves between each other. An electrical current is produced when he speaks into the microphone. Electrical current is created and transmitted to the other walkie-talkie which then converts it into sound waves alternating current

[Total 6 marks]

Exam Practice Tip

In the exams, you may be asked to explain why a given electromagnetic wave is suited to a particular use. So make sure you understand the properties of the different electromagnetic wave types, and know some of their most common uses.

Absorbing and Emitting Radiation

1 An object's temperature depends on how much radiation it is absorbing and emitting.

a) An object is absorbing the same amount of radiation as it is emitting.
State what is happening to the temperature of this object.

......0°C........It is......constant..........................

[1]

b) Compare the amount of radiation being absorbed and emitted by an object that is cooling down.

.....The.....object s.....absorb.....more.....radiation.............

....

[1]

[Total 2 marks]

2 The table below shows the temperatures of three different stars, A, B and C. The graph to the right of the table shows how the intensity of the radiation emitted by star A varies with wavelength.

Star	Temperature / °C
A	5500
B	4000
C	7000

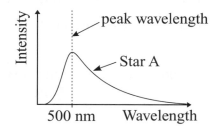

a) Which of the graphs below shows the correct intensity-wavelength distributions of stars B and C? The peak wavelength of star A is marked by the dotted line.

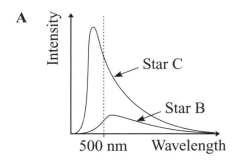

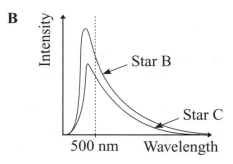

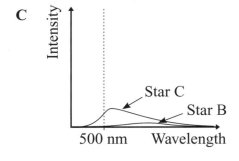

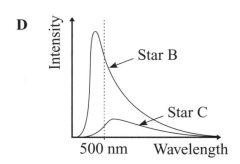

Answer ....

[1]

Chapter P1 — Radiation and Waves

b) Stars A, B and C all have their peak wavelengths in the visible spectrum.
Red light has the longest wavelength of all light in the visible spectrum.
Suggest which star's peak wavelength corresponds to red light.
Explain your reasoning with reference to the temperature of the stars.

....

....

....

[2]

[Total 3 marks]

3 Electromagnetic radiation from the Sun affects the temperature of the Earth. **Grade 6-7**

a) The Sun emits infrared radiation. Some of this radiation is incident upon the Earth.
Which of the following statements are **true (T)**, and which are **false (F)**?
Place a tick (✓) in the correct boxes.

	T	F
The atmosphere does not absorb infrared radiation.	✓	
The atmosphere reflects some infrared radiation.		✓
Infrared radiation cannot pass through the atmosphere.		✓
The atmosphere emits some infrared radiation.	✓	

[2]

b) The diagram below shows the Earth at two different times during a 24 hour period. A point on the Earth's surface is labelled **P**. At **Time 1**, it is daytime at point **P**. At **Time 2**, it is night-time at **P**.

Time 1   **Time 2**

Radiation from the Sun → P Earth   Radiation from the Sun → P Earth

Explain why the local temperature of point **P** on the Earth
is increasing at **Time 1**, and decreasing at **Time 2**.

During the day lots of EM
radiation is given to the
Earth by the Sun which
is absorbed by the atmosphere
through the surface

....

....

....

....

[4]

[Total 6 marks]

The Greenhouse Effect

1 The greenhouse effect is caused by greenhouse gases in the Earth's atmosphere. *(Grade 4-6)*

a) Which of the following is a greenhouse gas?
Place a tick (✓) in the box next to the correct answer.

helium ☐   nitrogen ☐   methane ☑   argon ☐

[1]

b) Give **one** human activity which has led to an increase in greenhouse gases in the atmosphere.
Explain how the human activity has caused this increase.

Burning of fossil fuels from the
fuel of cars can increase the
level of CO_2

[2]

[Total 3 marks]

2 Isaac is looking for information about climate change. *(Grade 7-9)*

a) Explain how atmospheric carbon dioxide affects the Earth's temperature.

Green gas gases absorb
a high amount of radiation

[2]

Isaac finds the graph on the right, which shows how atmospheric carbon dioxide concentration and temperature have changed over time. He states:

> This graph proves that an increased atmospheric carbon dioxide level causes global warming.

b) Use the graph and your understanding of correlation and cause to evaluate his statement.

It has the lower temperature to
its peak wavelength must be
the longest

[4]

[Total 6 marks]

Reflection and Ray Diagrams

Warm-Up

Complete the diagram below to show the path of the light ray through the reflective passage.

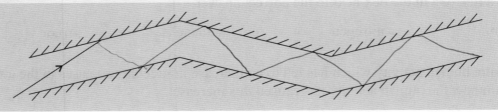

1 Yousef investigated the reflection of light by different types of surface. He used a flat, smooth mirror to reflect a light beam onto a piece of white card.

a) Predict the type of reflection which was observed at the mirror.

....

[1]

b) Yousef observed that the card did not reflect a clear beam of light. Explain why.

....

....

....

[3]

[Total 4 marks]

2 Two rays of light hit a mirror and are reflected. The diagram on the right shows the paths of the two reflected rays.

Which diagram below correctly shows the paths of the incident rays?

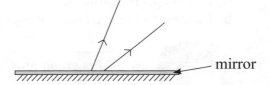

A

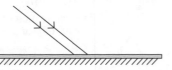

B

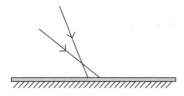

C

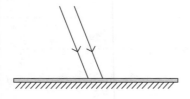

D

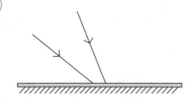

Answer ....

[Total 1 mark]

Refraction, Ray Diagrams and Prisms

1   A student shines a beam of white light through a block of clear plastic. The path of the light beam is shown in the diagram below.

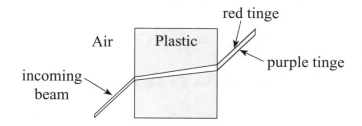

The student notices that the emergent beam is wider and is not pure white.
One side of the emergent beam has a red tinge, whilst the other side looks slightly purple.
Explain why this has happened.

....

....

....

....

....

....

[Total 4 marks]

2   You can use ray diagrams to show how light refracts as it passes through different substances.

Two parallel rays of light, one red and one blue, are directed towards a glass prism, as shown below. The rays are both transmitted by the prism.

On the diagram below, sketch the path taken by each ray as it travels through the prism, and out of the prism.

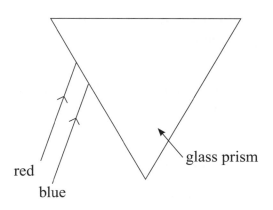

[Total 3 marks]

Exam Practice Tip

Remember, whenever you're drawing ray diagrams for mirrors or prisms, you should always draw in a dotted normal to any boundary the ray meets, at the point the ray meets it. This makes it a lot easier to judge whether your ray is going along the normal or at an angle to it, so you can figure out what will happen to it.

Lenses

Draw lines to connect each statement to the correct lens.

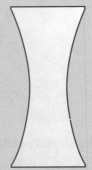

Usually called a concave lens.

Usually called a convex lens.

Brings parallel rays together to a point.

Spreads parallel rays out.

1   Lenses can be used refract light.
The diagram below shows a concave lens.
The principal focuses of the lens are labelled F.

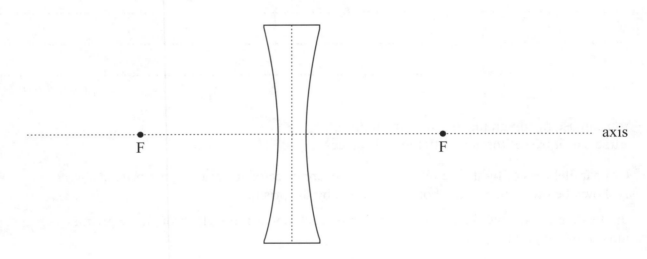

axis

F   F

a) On the diagram above, draw the path taken by a ray coming from the left,
parallel to the axis and passing through the lens.

[2]

b) Lenses can be used to produce images of objects. Which of the following statements is **true**?
Place a tick (✓) in the box next to the correct answer.

Only convex lenses can produce images.   ☐

Images are always produced on the opposite side of the lens to the object.   ☐

Images are always the same size as the object.   ☐

Both concave and convex lenses can produce images.   ☐

[1]

[Total 3 marks]

2 Ray diagrams are used to show how lenses produce images.
Complete the ray diagram below to show the image of the object formed
by the concave lens. The points marked F are the focal points of the lens.

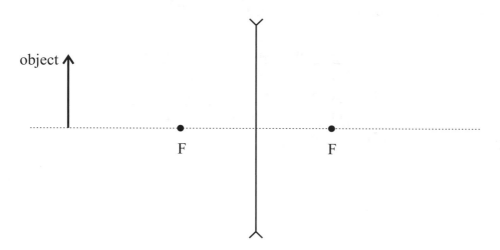

[Total 4 marks]

3 Rabia uses a convex lens to create an image of a pencil.

a) Complete the ray diagram below to show how the image is formed by the lens.
The points marked F are the focal points of the lens.

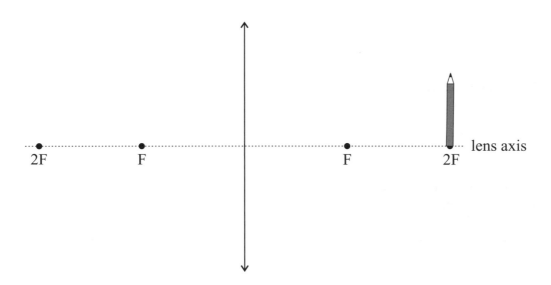

[4]

b) Rabia then replaces the convex lens with a concave lens.
Give **one** way in which the image of the pencil will change.

....

[1]

[Total 5 marks]

Exam Practice Tip

You can find the position of an image by drawing only two light rays. Don't spend lots of time trying to draw more.
And make sure that you draw your ray diagrams with a sharp pencil so they're clear and you can easily correct mistakes.

        Chapter P1 — Radiation and Waves

Visible Light and Colour

1 Which row in the table below correctly shows three colours of light in order of increasing frequency?

	← increasing frequency →		
A	red	blue	green
B	yellow	red	violet
C	blue	green	yellow
D	orange	green	violet

Answer ....

[Total 1 mark]

2 Nikolai is investigating the effect of coloured filters on the appearance of different objects.

Nikolai sets up the equipment below, then blocks out all other sources of light in the room.

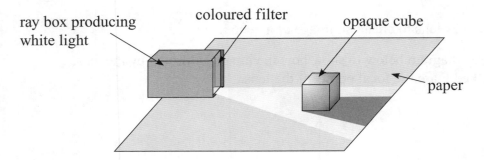

a) Nikolai places a white cube on the paper and a red filter in front of the ray box.
State the colour that the cube appears.

....

[1]

b) Nikolai replaces the white cube with a blue one.
State the colour the cube appears now. Explain your answer.

....

....

....

....

[3]

c) State what would happen if Nikolai were to add a blue filter to the ray box,
in front of the red filter.

....

[1]

[Total 5 marks]

Chapter P1 — Radiation and Waves

Sound Waves

Complete the passage below about sound waves, using the correct words from the list on the left. You don't have to use every word, and you can use the same word twice.

increases

decreases

stays the same

When a sound wave passes from air into a solid, its speed .... ,

the frequency of the sound wave .... and

the wavelength of the sound wave ....

1 The human ear is specialised to detect sound waves. **Grade 4-6**

a) Give the frequency range within which human ears transmit sound most efficiently.

....

[1]

b) Describe the function of the small bones in the middle ear.

....

....

[1]

[Total 2 marks]

2 Two children have made a toy telephone out of plastic pots and a piece of string. The string is tied to the bases of the pots and is pulled tight, as shown below. A child speaking into one pot can be heard by the child at the other end. **Grade 4-6**

When the first child speaks into their pot, a sound wave is produced in the air inside the pot. When the sound wave reaches the string at the bottom of the pot, it is transmitted into the string.

sound in → | pot | ———— string ———— | pot | sound out →

Describe how the sound wave is transmitted through the string to the second pot. Your answer should refer to the movement of particles as the sound wave is transmitted.

....

....

....

....

....

....

[Total 3 marks]

Chapter P1 — Radiation and Waves

Ultrasound and SONAR

1 Which of the following happens when a pulse of
ultrasound waves hits a boundary between materials?
Place a tick (✓) in the box next to the correct answer.   *Grade 4-6*

All of the waves are absorbed by the material. ☐

Some waves are reflected and the rest are transmitted into the material. ☐

The waves are transmitted and their frequency increases. ☐

The waves are transmitted and their frequency decreases. ☐

[Total 1 mark]

2 Describe how ultrasound can be used to produce an image of a person's kidneys.   *Grade 6-7*

....

....

....

....

[Total 3 marks]

3 A military ship is using SONAR to search for submarines.   *Grade 7-9*

a) The depth of the seabed in the area is known to be 1600 m. The speed of sound in seawater is
1520 m/s. The ship sends out an ultrasound wave and detects a reflected pulse 1.05 s later.

State whether this suggests that there may be a submarine beneath the ship.
You **must** support your answer with a calculation.

....

....

....

....

....

....

[4]

b) Suggest **one** way that a submarine could be made more difficult to detect with SONAR.
Give a reason for your answer.

....

....

....

[2]

[Total 6 marks]

Seismic Waves

1   Which of the following seismic waves only travel across the surface of the Earth? Place a tick (✓) in the box next to the correct answer.

Grade 4-6

S-waves   ☐

L-waves   ☐

P-waves   ☐

All of the above   ☐

[Total 1 mark]

2   To the right is a picture of the Earth. Seismic waves are being produced at point A. Two seismometers are positioned at points B and C. At B, both S-waves and P-waves are detected, but at C only P-waves are detected.

Grade 6-7

a) Explain how this indicates that part of the Earth's core is made from liquid.

....

....

....

[2]

b) The graph shows how the velocity of a P-wave changes as it travels through the Earth. Explain why the velocity of the wave suddenly changes at depths X and Y.

....

....

....

....

....

[4]

[Total 6 marks]

Exam Practice Tip

Sometimes, you'll be asked to answer a question using data given to you in the exam. Make sure that whatever you write down can be supported by the data you're given. Don't just write down what you think the answer should be from your revision — even if it's true, it may not be what the question was asking for.

Chapter P1 — Radiation and Waves

Chapter P2 — Sustainable Energy
Energy Stores and Transfers

Warm-Up

For each example, name the type of energy store that energy is being transferred away from.

1) A skydiver falling from an aeroplane. ....

2) A substance undergoing a nuclear reaction. ....

3) A stretched rubber band springing back to its original shape. ....

4) A piece of burning coal. ....

1 A kettle of cold water is plugged into the mains and brought to the boil. Energy is transferred from the mains to the water. *(Grade 4-6)*

a) Name the energy store of the water that the energy is transferred **to**.

    Potential energy n Thermal

[1]

b) Place a tick (✓) in the box next to the statement that is **true**.

The work done by the electric current is equal to half the energy transferred to the kettle. ☐

The work done by the electric current is equal to the energy transferred to the kettle. ☑

The work done by the electric current is equal to double the energy transferred to the kettle. ☐

No work is done as energy is transferred to the kettle. ☐

[1]

[Total 2 marks]

2 Sonja is riding her bike. She takes her feet off the pedals to freewheel down a hill. *(Grade 4-6)*

Describe the energy transfers that take place as the bike travels down the hill.
Ignore friction and air resistance.

    There would be a lot of kinetic
    energy. There would be potential
    energy building up as you go up the
    hill and when you go down there is
    kinetic energy.

[Total 3 marks]

Exam Practice Tip

Make sure you know the different types of energy store and remember that energy transfers can occur mechanically (because of a force doing work), electrically (by moving charges), by heating or by radiation (e.g. light and sound waves).

Conservation of Energy and Power

1 A hot potato is placed in a cool room. The room and potato are assumed to be a closed system. Place a tick (✓) in the box next to the statement which is **true**.

All of the energy in the thermal energy store of the hot potato is transferred to the thermal energy store of the room. ☐

All of the energy in the thermal energy store of the room is transferred to the thermal energy store of the hot potato. ☑

Some of the energy in the thermal energy store of the hot potato is dissipated to the thermal energy store of the room. ☑

No energy transfers occur between the thermal energy stores of hot potato and the room. ☐

[Total 1 mark]

2 A student is investigating the work done by different washing machines during a standard washing cycle. The table below shows the manufacturer's data about three machines.

Machine	Power	Time needed
A	600 W	125 minutes
B	400 W	165 minutes
C	500w	125 minutes

a) Calculate the work done by machine A during its standard washing cycle. Give your answer in kJ.

?

Work done = ...13°.0.......... kJ
[4]

b) Machine C's standard cycle lasts for 125 minutes. It does 3 930 000 J of work in that time. Complete the table above by calculating the power of machine C.

125 mins   2hms 5min
3,930,000 J
[2]

c) The price of electricity is 16p per kWh. A homeowner uses washing machine B once a week on its standard cycle. Calculate the cost in pounds of using washing machine B for a year. Give your answer to the nearest penny.

pt 16p per kwh

Price = £ ..4.4......
[4]
[Total 10 marks]

Chapter P2 — Sustainable Energy

Efficiency and Sankey Diagrams

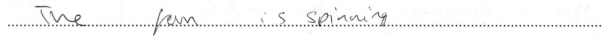

1   An electric fan transfers 7500 J of energy. 2 kJ of this is wasted energy.

a) Suggest **one** way in which energy is wasted by the fan.

.............The..........fan............is spinning...

[1]

b) Draw a Sankey diagram for the electric fan on the grid below.

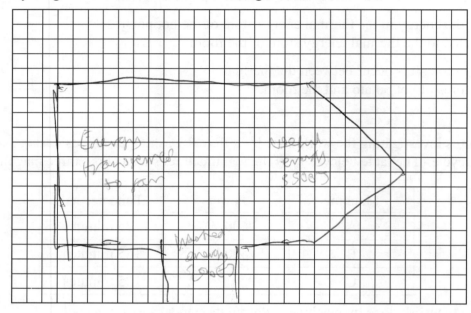

[3]

c) Calculate the efficiency of the fan. Give your answer as a decimal to **two** significant figures.

Efficiency = ...
[2]

[Total 6 marks]

2   An electric kettle has an efficiency of 76%. 2500 J of energy is transferred from the mains to the kettle every second. When the kettle is full, it needs to transfer 418 000 J of energy to the thermal energy store of the water to boil it.

Calculate how long a full kettle needs to be switched on for in order to boil the water.

Time = ... s
[Total 4 marks]

Energy Resources

Write the energy resources below in the correct column to show whether they are renewable or non-renewable.

biofuel   hydroelectricity

oil

solar   nuclear fuel

coal

tidal   natural gas

Renewable	Non-renewable
Solar hydroelectricity	Coal

1   The amount of electricity generated by wind turbines is increasing in the UK.   Grade 4-6

a) State whether wind is a renewable or non-renewable energy resource. Explain why.

Wind is a renewable energy source. You can use it again and again.

[2]

b) Describe how wind turbines generate electricity.

Wind turbines spin causing electricity

[2]

[Total 4 marks]

2   Electricity can be generated by burning biofuels, such as animal waste collected from farms or specially grown crops like sugar cane.   Grade 6-7

Describe the process by which biofuels can be used to generate electricity.

Biofuels can be reused and are an essential source of energy. I am running. Biofuels can be made from waste biofuels and like fossil fuels

[Total 5 marks]

3 An energy provider is thinking about replacing their old fossil fuel power station. They are eligible for a government grant, so the initial building costs are negligible. Stephen and Max are discussing whether it is worth replacing the old power station.

Stephen
I think it's better to keep using fossil fuels. The most important thing is that people have a reliable electricity supply. A fossil fuel power station can provide this.

Max
But using fossil fuels to generate electricity isn't sustainable. We should switch to a renewable resource.

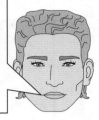

a) Explain what Stephen and Max mean by their statements. In your answer you should compare the reliability and sustainability of fossil fuels and renewable energy resources.

the gas Fossil fuels can
harm our planet and it
can lead to global
warming. Ice caps are
melting a ismitimg. Wine
is renewable

[4]

b) The energy provider decides to replace the old power station with either a hydroelectric power (HEP) station or a tidal barrage. Both of these use renewable energy. Compare generating electricity using these two energy resources. In your answer you should comment on their running and fuel costs, their reliability and their impact on the environment.

You can assume the initial building costs of both types will be covered by the government grant.

If it is renewable
energy random ity
good for the environment
isn't and will
you reduce climate
change.

[5]

[Total 9 marks]

Trends in Energy Use

1   The bar chart below shows the electricity generated from renewable and non-renewable energy sources in a small country over 20 years.

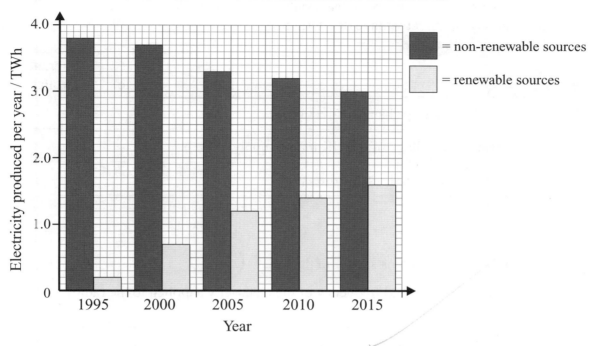

a) How much **more** electricity did the country produce per year in 2015 than in 1995?

0·6

..................1500.................. TWh

[2]

b)* Describe the trends in total electricity production and in the type of energy sources used shown by the bar chart. Suggest reasons for these trends. Use data from the graph in your answer.

There is a negative trend. Non renewable resources are decreasing. However, renewable sources are actually aramically increasing which is actually a good thing. This will limit climate change.

[6]

[Total 8 marks]

The National Grid

In the table below, put a tick next to each statement to show whether it applies to direct voltage or alternating voltage.

	Direct voltage	Alternating voltage
It constantly changes direction.		✓
It describes the voltage of the UK mains supply.		✓
It is always in the same direction.	✓	

1 A radio is connected to the mains supply in the UK. Grade 4-6

a) State the potential difference and frequency of the electricity supplied to the radio.

....

[1]

b) The cable connecting the radio to the mains contains a live wire, a neutral wire and an earth wire. Give the sizes of the potential differences between:

i) the live wire and the neutral wire

.... 5o V
[1]

ii) the neutral wire and the earth wire

.... too V
[1]

[Total 3 marks]

2 Complete the following table to show whether each statement about the national grid is **true** or **false**. Place a tick (✓) in the correct boxes. 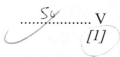 Grade 4-6

Statement	True	False
Transformers increase the size of the electrical current before it is transferred through the national grid.	✓	
Transferring electricity through the national grid at high p.d. reduces energy loss.		✓
Transformers decrease the p.d. of electricity from the national grid before it reaches homes and businesses.	✓	

[Total 2 marks]

3 The cable that connects an iron to the mains supply has become worn with use. Both the cable insulation and live wire insulation have become worn, as shown in the diagram below.

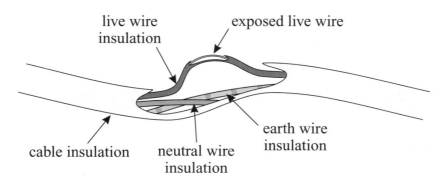

a) Tim plugs in the iron and switches it on. He accidentally touches the exposed live wire and receives an electric shock. Explain why he receives an electric shock. You should refer to the electrical potential of Tim in your answer.

The ~~etc~~ electrical potential of Tim could be higher ~~th~~ than electrical potential. He got an electric shock.

[3]

b) The socket is switched off and the iron is unplugged.
Tim makes the following statement:

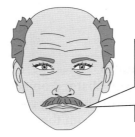

Tim
There is no danger of receiving an electric shock from the plug socket.

Explain whether Tim is right or wrong.

Tim is wrong as there is a risk of getting an electrical shock

[2]

[Total 5 marks]

Exam Practice Tip

If you get a question asking about the danger of touching live wires, you should always make sure your explanation includes the electric potential of the live wire and the electric potential of the object touching it.

Chapter P2 — Sustainable Energy

Chapter P3 — Electric Circuits

Static Electricity

1 A man walks up some carpeted stairs. The carpet and the man's shoes rub together, making the man electrically charged. The handrail along the stairs is made of metal and is electrically connected to earth. When the man puts his hand near the rail, there is a spark.

(Grade 4-6)

a) Describe what is happening during the spark.

Metals conduct electricity Electrons jump across the gap between the rail and the man.

[1]

b) The spark leapt from the man to the handrail.
State whether the man was positively or negatively charged.

Positive x Negative.

[1]

[Total 2 marks]

2 A plastic polythene rod is hanging by a string, as shown in the diagram. It is rubbed with a cloth. A negative static charge builds up on the rod.

(Grade 4-6)

a) Explain how a static charge builds up on the rod.

cloth rod
Electrons move from the plastic onto the cloth.
The cloth then has a negative charge. So, The rod
gained
lost electrons and it has a positive negative charge.

[2]

b) Some students are predicting what will happen if other charged objects are placed near the rod. Lauren makes the following statement:

Lauren
If another negatively charged object is brought close to the hanging rod, the rod will swing away from the object.

State whether Lauren is correct or not. Explain why, with reference to electric fields.

She is correct Correct as opposite charges attract
negative
eachother, not repel. The rod has a positive charge
meaning it can attract negatively charged objects will
repel negative charged objects. then Both objects have
an electrical field when their fields interact, there is
a force on both objects.

[3]

[Total 5 marks]

Exam Practice Tip

Remember — all electrically charged objects generate an electric field. The strength of this field depends on the size of the charge and how far away from it you are. The closer you are, or the bigger the charge, the stronger the field.

Circuits — The Basics

Fill in the blanks in these sentences with the words below.
You don't have to use every word, but each word can only be used once.

............Current.................. is the rate of flow of electric charge around a circuit.

A current will flow around a circuit if the circuit is ....closed.............. and

there is a source of ....potential difference.......... .

coulomb	open	current
potential difference	resistance	closed

1 The figure below shows the circuit symbol for a variable resistor. (Grade 4-6)

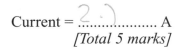

a) Draw a circuit diagram of a circuit made up of a battery, a filament lamp, and a variable resistor, connected on a single, closed loop of wire.

[3]

b) The variable resistor can be used to change the resistance of the circuit.
Describe how increasing the resistance of the variable resistor will affect the potential difference across the circuit and the current through the circuit.

...The p.d remains the same...

....

[2]

[Total 5 marks]

2 A simple circuit contains a battery and a resistor. (Grade 6-7)
Over 3.0 hours, 29 000 C of charge passes through the resistor.

Calculate the current flowing through the circuit during this time.
Give your answer to **two** significant figures.

Current = ...2.7...... A

[Total 5 marks]

Resistance and $V = I \times R$

1 A direct current of 3.0 A flows through a circuit consisting of a battery and a 6.0 Ω resistor. Calculate the potential difference across the resistor.

 Grade 4-6

$V = I \times R$

3×6

$= 18$

Potential difference = ...18...... V

[Total 3 marks]

2 Jackie investigated how the resistance of a piece of wire depends on its length. The circuit she used is shown in the diagram below. Her results are displayed in the table.

 Grade 6-7

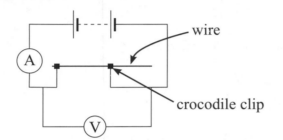

Length / cm	Resistance / Ω
10	0.6
20	1.3
30	1.7
40	2.4
50	3.0

a) Describe how Jackie could have used the apparatus above to obtain her results.

Could have varied the length of the wire between the crocodile clips.

[2]

b) Plot the data given in the table on the grid and axes below. Draw a line of best fit for the data.

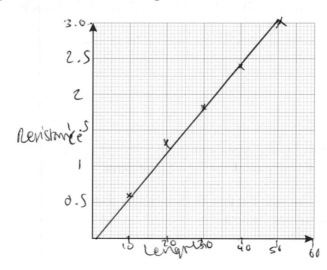

[4]

c) Using your line of best fit, determine the resistance of the wire for a length of 25 cm.

Resistance for 25 cm = ... Ω

[1]

[Total 7 marks]

Resistance and *I-V* Characteristics

1   Viktor is investigating the *I-V* characteristics of various circuit components.   (Grade 4-6)

   a)   Viktor starts by investigating the *I-V* characteristic of a filament lamp.
Which of the graphs below correctly shows the *I-V* characteristic for a filament lamp?

     A   **B**   **C**   **D**

Answer ......B........

[1]

   b)   Viktor then tests a fixed resistor. A fixed resistor is a linear component. Explain what is meant by a '**linear component**'. Describe the shape of a linear component's *I-V* characteristic.

A linear component is a component with a constant resistance. The I-V characteristic of a linear component is a straight line.

[2]

[Total 3 marks]

PRACTICAL

2*   James is investigating the resistance of a diode.   (Grade 7-9)

James uses the circuit shown on the right to investigate how the resistance of the diode changes with the current. Describe how James could use this circuit to plot an *I-V* characteristic for the diode. Explain how he should ensure he gets a valid set of results.

....

....

....

....

....

....

....

....

....

[Total 6 marks]

Circuit Devices

1 Sophia wants to investigate how the resistance of an LDR changes with light intensity.

a) Draw a circuit diagram (including an ammeter and a voltmeter) of a circuit that could be used to measure the resistance of an LDR.

[3]

b) Sophia varies the intensity of the light hitting the LDR by partly covering it with a piece of paper. She covers the LDR with the paper by varying amounts, and calculates the resistance each time. Her results are shown in the table below.

Percentage of resistor covered	Resistance (Ω)
0%	800
25%	1000
50%	1300
75%	1800

Describe what Sophia's results show about the relationship between the light intensity the LDR is exposed to and its resistance.

Resistance increases per resistor covered
Resistance of LDR the increases as Light intensity
decreases

[1]

[Total 4 marks]

2 Mark builds the sensing circuit shown on the right and places it next to an electric hob. He turns the electric hob on and uses the circuit to see when the hob is hot.

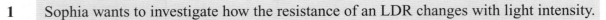

a) Describe how the circuit works.

When the temperature is low, the resistance
is high. So current is small and the
lamp is dim

[4]

b) Suggest **one** limitation of Mark using this circuit to see when the hob is hot.

The circuit will not give Mark the
actual temperature.

[1]

[Total 5 marks]

Energy and Power in Circuits

For each statement, circle whether it is true or false.

Potential difference is the work done per unit charge.   (True) / False

One volt is one ampere per coulomb.   True / (False)

Electrical charge in a current does work against resistance.   (True) / False

---

1   A circuit component has a power rating of 0.015 kW. Grade 4-6

a) Describe what is meant by the '**power rating**' of a circuit component.

How much energy is transferred to the component per second.

[1]

b) Calculate the energy transferred to the component when operating at its power rating for 10.0 hours. Give your answer in **joules**.

Power = 0.015 × 1000 = 15W

time = 10 × 60 × 60 = 36000

energy transferred = power × time

= 540,000J

Energy = 540,000 J

[4]

[Total 5 marks]

---

2   A kettle does a total of 2.76×10^5 J of work to bring water to the boil. It is connected to the mains supply which has a voltage of 230 V. Grade 6-7

a) Calculate the total charge that passes through the kettle in the time it takes to boil the water.

pd = work done / charge

charge = wd / p.d

$(2.76 \times 10^5) \div 230$

= 1200

Charge = 1200 C

[3]

b) A toaster is connected to the same mains supply. During the time it takes to toast a slice of bread, the total charge that passes through the toaster is 980 C.

Calculate the energy transferred by the toaster in the time it takes to toast the slice of bread. Give your answer in **kilojoules** and to **three** significant figures.

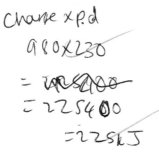

charge × p.d

980 × 230

= 225400

= 225400

= 225kJ

Energy transferred = 225 kJ

[4]

[Total 7 marks]

3 Fans use a motor to turn a set of blades. `Grade 6-7`

a) A 75 W ceiling fan in an office is powered by the mains supply at 230 V.
Calculate the current supplied to the fan. Give your answer to **two** significant figures.

Power = p.d × current

current = power / p.d

$I = \dfrac{\cancel{P}}{R}$ = $\sqrt{\dfrac{230}{3.06}}$

$R = \dfrac{V}{I}$ $R = \dfrac{V}{I} = \dfrac{230}{75} = 3.06\,\Omega$

= $\dfrac{75}{230}$ = 0.326

Current = 0.33 A   [4]

b) Describe the energy transfers that occur whilst the ceiling fan is on,
starting from the mains electricity, to the blades of the fan.

Energy is transferred to the mains
supply electrically

[3]

c) A small desk fan runs from a computer's USB port. It has a power of 2.45 W, and draws
a current of 0.350 A. Calculate its resistance.

$R = \dfrac{V}{I}$ $\dfrac{2.45}{0.350}$

= 0

power = current² × resistance

resistance = power / current²

= $\dfrac{2.45}{0.350^2}$ = 20

Resistance = 20 Ω   [3]

[Total 10 marks]

4 A child is playing with a toy car. The car is powered by a
6.0 V battery and has two speed settings — fast and slow. `Grade 7-9`

a) The child sets the speed to slow and drives the car for 76 seconds. During this time, the car
transfers 720 J of energy. Calculate the current through the car when it is being driven.

$I = \dfrac{V}{R}$

V = 6.0
I = ?
R = ?

Power = energy transferred / time

= $\dfrac{720}{76}$ = 9.4736 W

power = p.d × current

current = power / p.d   = $\dfrac{9.4736}{6}$ = 1.578

= 1.6 A

Current = 1.6 A   [5]

b) The child now sets the speed to fast. The power of the car at this speed is 15 W.
Explain why the battery runs down more quickly when the car is set at a higher speed.

[2]

[Total 7 marks]

Series and Parallel Circuits

1 The diagrams below show four different circuits.

Which of the diagrams below shows all the components connected in series?

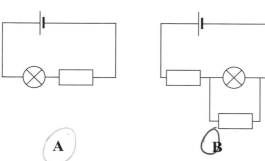

A   B   C   D

Answer ....

[Total 1 mark]

2 The diagram on the right shows a series circuit containing two resistors and a cell.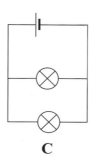

Calculate the potential difference across the 30.0 Ω resistor.

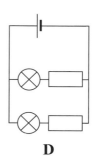

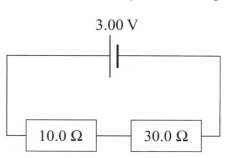

3.00 V

10.0 Ω   30.0 Ω

$$10 + 30 = 40$$

$$3 \div 40$$

$$= 0.075A \qquad 0.075 \times 30$$

Potential difference = ...2.25....... V

[Total 5 marks]

3* Explain why adding resistors in series with each other increases the total resistance of the resistors, whilst adding resistors in parallel with each other decreases the total resistance of the resistors.

The more the resistors that are in a series, the lower the potential difference across each one. So there would be lower current through each resistor. There would be lower potential difference in the resistors.

[Total 6 marks]

Chapter P3 — Electric Circuits

Investigating Series and Parallel Circuits

1   Doris is investigating the properties of series and parallel circuits, using bulbs which are labelled as having the same resistance. Doris sets up **Circuit 1**.

Grade 6-7

The voltmeter reads 12 V and the ammeter reads 0.25 A.
Doris uses these values to calculate the resistance of each bulb.

a) Calculate the resistance of each bulb, assuming that the bulbs do have the same resistance.

Circuit 1

Bulb 1   Bulb 2

$R = \dfrac{V}{I} = \dfrac{V}{I \times R}$ $\dfrac{12}{0.25}$ Resistance of BOTH $= \dfrac{48}{2} = 24$

$\dfrac{V}{I}$

Resistance = ~~48~~ 24 .... Ω
[3]

b) Doris then adds a third bulb to the circuit, and makes **Circuit 2**.

i) Assuming that bulb 3 is identical to bulbs 1 and 2, calculate the new current through the ammeter.

$\dfrac{12}{24} = 0.5$ $0.5 + 0.25$
$= 0.75 \quad 0.75A$

Circuit 2

Bulb 1   Bulb 2

Bulb 3

Current = ...0.75...... A
[3]

ii) Doris observes that bulb 3 is brighter than bulbs 1 and 2. Explain why.

More current goes to bulb 3. 1 and 2 share the source potential difference.

[2]

c) Doris then adds a resistor to **Circuit 2** in series with bulb 3.

i) State the effect of this on the current through the ammeter.

Current through ammeter decreases.

[1]

ii) State how this affects the brightness of the three bulbs.

It will increase due to higher current. Bulb 1 and 2 dont change. Bulb 3 gets dimmer

[2]

[Total 11 marks]

Exam Practice Tip

You might get a question like this one where some components are connected in series with each other, but there's more than one branch to the circuit. Don't panic, just remember that the rules for parallel circuits apply when you're looking at the different branches, and the rules for series circuits apply when you're looking at the components on one branch.

Permanent and Induced Magnets

For each statement, circle whether it is true (T) or false (F).

A magnetic field is a region where other magnets experience a force. Ⓣ/ F

Field lines show in which direction a force would act on a south pole at that point. Ⓣ/Ⓕ

The further away from a magnet you get, the weaker its magnetic field is. T /Ⓕ

1 All magnets produce magnetic fields. (Grade 4-6)

a) Which of the following statements about magnets is **correct**?
Place a tick (✓) in the box next to the correct answer.

Like poles attract each other. ☐

Magnetic fields are weakest at the poles of a magnet. ☐

Unlike poles attract each other. ☑

Iron is not a magnetic material. ☐

[1]

b) Field lines can be used to represent the magnetic field around a magnet.
Place a tick (✓) in the box next to the **true** statement about magnetic field lines.

They always point from a south pole to a north pole. ☐

They are used to show which direction a charged particle would move in the field. ☐

They can only be straight lines. ☑

They are closer together where the magnetic field is stronger. ☐

[1]

c) Two bar magnets are held near to each other, as shown in the diagram below.
The diagram shows some of the field lines in the region between the two magnets.

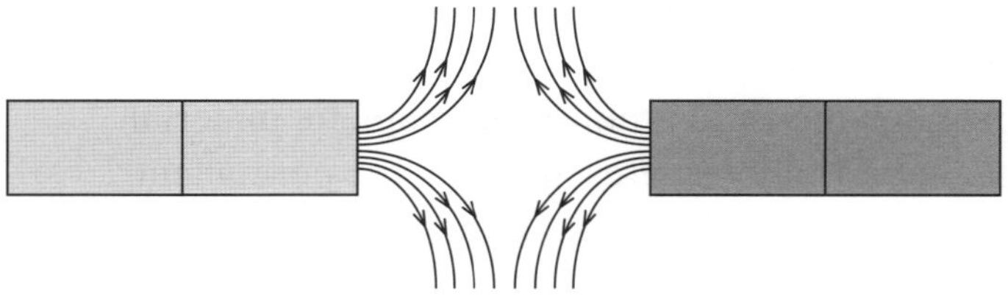

State the behaviour of the two magnets once they are released. Explain your answer.

They completely repel away from
eachother due to the same poles facing
eachother. For ce is repuling. A force is
acting on both magnen due to their interacting
magnetic fields.

[3]

[Total 5 marks]

2 Magnetic compasses are used for navigation. They contain a small bar magnet.

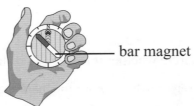

—— bar magnet

Describe the behaviour of a magnetic compass when it is far away from other magnets. Explain how this behaviour provides evidence that the Earth's core is magnetic.

When a compass is far from other magnets, the north pole of a compass needle points towards the Earth's magnetic north pole. This suggests the Earth has a magnetic field.

[Total 3 marks]

3 The diagram below shows two bars. One is a permanent magnet. One is made from a magnetic material. The magnetic field pattern around the bars is shown.

a) There is a force of attraction between the two bars. Add labels to show the poles on both bars, and arrows to the field lines, to complete the diagram. One of the poles has been labelled for you.

Permanent bar magnet   Magnetic material

N

[3]

b) The permanent magnet is removed.
There is no longer a magnetic field around the magnetic material.
Explain why the magnetic field was present when the permanent magnet was present, but not after it had been removed.

Magnetic fields occur when two magnets meet. Since there is no other magnet present there is not any forces of attraction. because induced magnet is had its own magnetic force field.

[2]

[Total 5 marks]

Chapter P3 — Electric Circuits

Electromagnetism

1   A student creates a solenoid, as shown below.

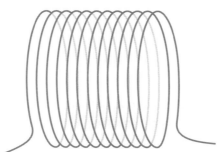

a)   Explain the effect winding a current-carrying wire into a solenoid
     will have on the magnetic field around the wire.

     The magnetic field around the loop of wire
     add together. This causes the strength of the
     magnetic field to increase.   [2]

b)   Which of the following statements about a current-carrying solenoid is **true**?
     Place a tick (✓) in the box next to the correct answer.

     It is not possible to change the strength of the magnetic field around a solenoid.   ☐

     The strength of the magnetic field produced increases with distance from the solenoid.   ☐

     If the current is stopped, there will no longer be a magnetic field around the solenoid.   ☑

     The direction of the magnetic field does not depend on the direction of the current.   ☐
                                                                                        [1]

c)   The student then added an iron core to the solenoid to create an electromagnet. State what effect,
     if any, this has on the strength of the magnetic field produced by the current through the wire.

     Strength increased.   [1]

d)   State **one** difference between the magnetic properties of permanent magnets and electromagnets.
     permanent magnet always has a magnetic field but an
     electricity revolves be a an electromagnet but an
     electromagnet can be turned on and off.   [1]

e)   Describe how the student could show the presence of a magnetic field around the solenoid.

     ....

     ....

     ....
                                                                                        [2]
                                                                          [Total 7 marks]

2   The diagram below shows a wire which has a current flowing through it. The arrow shows the direction of the current.

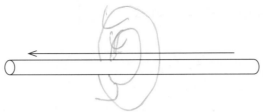

a) The flow of charge creates a magnetic field around the wire.
On the diagram, draw field lines showing the shape and direction of the magnetic field created.

[2]

b) The direction of the current is reversed. State the effect this will have on the magnetic field.

.... Direction of field is reversed ....

[1]

c) State **one** way in which the magnetic field strength around the wire could be increased.

.... Increases current ....

[1]

[Total 4 marks]

3   Louise is investigating electromagnets and their uses.

She states the following:

> **Louise**
> The discovery of the electromagnetic effect led to huge advances in communications.

Describe what Louise means and explain how this had a positive influence on people's lives.

.... EM relays were used to create ....
.... Telegraphs which are used for ....
Communication.

[Total 3 marks]

Exam Practice Tip

Electromagnetism can be a tough topic, but it has lots of practical applications, so make sure you know the properties of electromagnets well. Take your time reading through questions, especially ones that ask you to explain or describe something. Make sure your answer covers all the points that the question has told you to talk about.

The Motor Effect

Warm-Up

The diagram shows a left hand being used for Fleming's left hand rule. Using **three** of the labels below, label the thumb and fingers in the diagram with the quantities they represent.

Force

Magnetic field

Current

Current   Force
Voltage
Magnet
Wire
Magnetic field

1   A straight current-carrying wire inside a magnetic field experiences a force. The wire is at right angles to the magnetic field.   *(Grade 4-6)*

Place a tick (✓) in the box that describes how the size of this force could be increased.

By decreasing the length of the wire.   ☐

By decreasing the current through the wire.   ☑

By reversing the direction of the magnetic field.   ☑

By increasing the strength of the magnetic field.   ☑

[Total 1 mark]

2   A current-carrying wire is between two magnetic poles, shown below. The direction of the current is out of the paper.   *(Grade 4-6)*

a) The wire experiences a force.
   Draw the direction of the force acting on the wire on the diagram below.

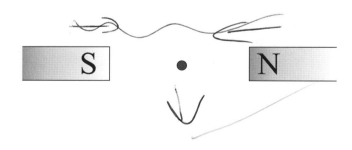

S   •   N

[1]

b) The direction of the current is reversed.
   State what effect this will have on the direction and size of the force acting on the wire.

It with reverse It will reverse (direction) size of force wont change

[2]

[Total 3 marks]

Chapter P3 — Electric Circuits

3 A 30.0 cm long current-carrying wire is placed between magnetic poles.

a) The magnetic flux density is 2.2 T and the current through the wire is 15 A.
Calculate the force acting on the wire.

2.2×15×0.3
=9.9

Force = ...9.9....... N
[3]

b) Explain why the wire experiences a force.

Two poles attract
Magnetic fields between poles and around poles interact
resulting in a force.
[1]

[Total 4 marks]

4 The diagram shows a current-carrying wire between two magnetic poles, with all objects drawn at their actual size. A current of 2.6 A is flowing through the wire, from left to right. A force of 0.0183 N is acting on the wire, directed out of the paper.

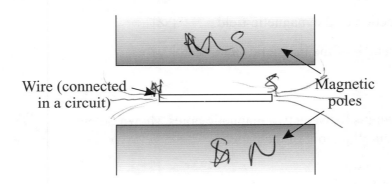

Wire (connected in a circuit) ... Magnetic poles

a) Complete the diagram by labelling each magnetic pole as a north or south pole.
[1]

b) Calculate the magnetic field strength between the poles.
Give your answer to **two** significant figures.

=0.0183÷(2.6×0.025)

=0.281538

=0.28 T

Magnetic field strength = ...0.28....... T
[5]

[Total 6 marks]

Exam Practice Tip

If you get stuck and can't remember the equation you need to use, have a look at the data sheet you'll be given in the exam (ours is on the back cover) — you may find one that helps you answer the question. If you don't, you should still write down any bits that you can do (like conversions) — you might get some marks for it.

Electric Motors

1 A simple direct current (d.c.) motor is shown in the diagram below. It consists of a magnetic north pole, a magnetic south pole and a rotating coil of wire connected to a circuit.

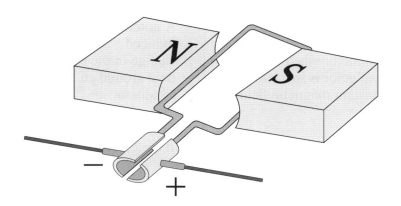

a) i) Describe how a simple d.c. motor works.

Direct current will only flow one direction. One side is North and the other is South.

[3]

ii) Give **one** way in which the direction of the coil's rotation can be reversed.

Swap magnetic poles.

[1]

b) The number of turns on the coil affects the speed of rotation of the motor.
State **two** other factors which determine the speed of rotation of the motor.

1. No Size of current through coil.

2. ....

[2]

c) Electric motors have many everyday applications.
The use of motors has had an impact on most areas of life.

Give **one** example of an everyday use of electric motors.
Suggest how this has had a positive impact on the situation in which the motor is used.

Motors that drive conveyer belts in factories

[2]

[Total 8 marks]

Chapter P3 — Electric Circuits

Electromagnetic Induction

1   Johan and Syed are discussing electromagnetic induction.

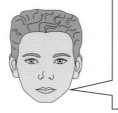

Johan
A potential difference is induced in an electrical conductor when the conductor is in a strong, constant magnetic field.

Syed
A potential difference is induced when there is a change in the magnetic field around an electrical conductor.

State whether Johan, Syed, both or neither of them are correct.

....

[Total 1 mark]

2   Natasha sets up a simple circuit to measure the current generated when she moves a magnet in and out of a coil. The set-up of her apparatus is shown below.

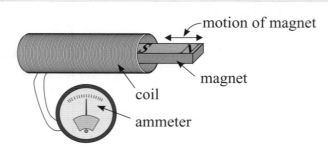

a)   State whether the set-up shown generates alternating or direct current. Explain your answer.

....

....

....

....

[3]

b)   When Natasha holds the bar magnet still inside the coil, there is no current recorded by the ammeter. Explain why.

....

....

[1]

[Total 4 marks]

Exam Practice Tip

As well as explaining what electromagnetic induction actually is, you might have to talk about its uses. Mains electricity is generated through electromagnetic induction and transmitted around the country with the help of transformers that also use electromagnetic induction. Electromagnetic induction also has applications in devices such as microphones.

Chapter P3 — Electric Circuits

Generators

1 A wind-up torch contains a dynamo. A handle on the side of the torch is attached to the coil in the dynamo. When the handle is turned, the torch bulb lights up.

a) Explain how turning the handle causes the bulb to light up.

....

....

....

[3]

b) The dynamo contains a split-ring commutator.
Describe the purpose of the split-ring commutator in the dynamo.

....

....

[1]

c) The current that the dynamo generates creates its own magnetic field.
Describe the direction that the magnetic field will be created in.

....

....

[1]

[Total 5 marks]

2 The diagram below shows a basic alternator. The graph shows the alternator's output potential difference (p.d.) trace when the wire is rotated. When the frequency of rotation of the wire is doubled, the output p.d. doubles. On the graph below, sketch the output p.d. trace when the frequency of rotation is doubled.

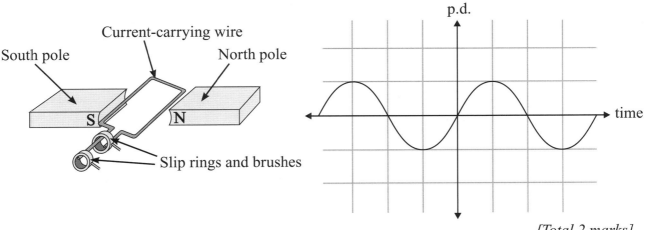

[Total 2 marks]

Exam Practice Tip

You need to be able to interpret potential difference-time graphs for both alternators and dynamos. Make sure you can recognise a p.d. trace. Remember, for direct potential differences, the p.d. trace isn't just a horizontal straight line — it still has peaks like an alternating p.d. trace, but it never crosses the time axis, since it's always going in the same direction.

Loudspeakers, Microphones & Transformers

Warm-Up

For each option, circle the word to correctly describe how loudspeakers work.

A(n) (alternating / direct) current is passed through a coil of wire that is wrapped around one pole of a (permanent / induced) magnet and attached to the base of a cone. When a current flows, the coil experiences a (force / moment) which makes the cone move.

1   The figure below shows the structure of a moving coil microphone.

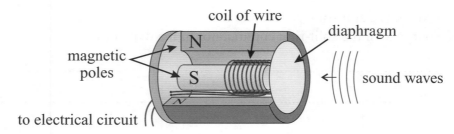

a) An end-view of the permanent magnet inside of the microphone is shown below.
Complete the diagram by drawing the magnetic field lines for the magnet within the microphone.

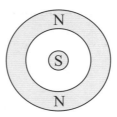

[2]

b) Explain how the microphone converts sound waves to electrical signals.

....
....
....
....
....
....

[4]

c) State the type of current produced by the microphone. Explain your answer.

....
....
....
....

[3]

[Total 9 marks]

Chapter P3 — Electric Circuits

2* Transformers use electromagnetic induction to increase or decrease the potential difference that is supplied to them.

Explain how a step-up transformer uses electromagnetic induction to increase its output potential difference. Your answer should refer to the number of turns on each coil of the transformer.

....

....

....

....

....

....

....

....

....

....

....

....

[Total 6 marks]

3 Keith is investigating how transformers work. He sets up the apparatus shown below.

power supply — primary coil — secondary coil — V

The power supply is set to provide direct current. When the power supply is switched on, there is a sudden increase in potential difference in the secondary coil, which quickly drops to zero. The potential difference in the secondary coil remains at zero while the power supply is on.

Explain Keith's observations, with reference to the magnetic field through the transformer.

....

....

....

....

....

....

[Total 3 marks]

Chapter P3 — Electric Circuits

More on Transformers

1 A transformer is made of two coils joined by an iron core. It has 75 turns in the secondary coil. An input p.d. of 72 V is converted to an output p.d. of 12 V.

Calculate the number of turns on the primary coil.

Number of turns = ...

[Total 3 marks]

2 A transformer is 100% efficient. The current through the primary coil is 20.0 A and the potential difference across it is 30.0 V. The potential difference across the secondary coil is 40.0 V. Calculate the current through the secondary coil.

Current = ... A

[Total 3 marks]

3 Electricity produced in power stations is transmitted to people's homes by the national grid. The national grid often transmits electricity at 400 000 V.

Describe the role of the transformers used to transmit electricity from a power station to the network. Explain how their use allows energy to be transferred efficiently across the national grid.

....

....

....

....

....

....

....

....

[Total 4 marks]

Exam Practice Tip

The equations you need for questions 1 and 2 will be given to you in the exam — you just have to choose the correct ones from the list. To work out which one to use, it might help to make a list of all the values you've been given.

Forces and Newton's Third Law

Warm-Up

Which of the following is Newton's Third Law? Tick **one** box.

A non-zero resultant force is needed to cause a change in speed or direction. ☐

A resultant force is inversely proportional to the mass of an object. ☐

When two objects interact, they exert equal and opposite forces on each other. ☑

A resultant force of zero leads to an equilibrium situation. ☐

1 Dave is at rest on his skateboard. He then pushes against a wall.
You can assume there is no friction between the skateboard and the ground.

(Grade 4-6)

a) Explain why Dave would move away from the wall.

As he applies force onto the wall, it pushes him
back resulting in him moving away from the wall.
The same force he exerted onto the wall pushed
him back.

[2]

b) State **one** contact force and **one** non-contact force that act on the skateboard.

Contact force: Friction

Non-contact force: Gravitational force

[2]

[Total 4 marks]

2 A plate in equilibrium is sitting on a table. Explain why $W_E = R_T$.

(Grade 7-9)

R_P = normal contact force of table pushing up on plate
R_T = normal contact force of plate pushing down on table
W_P = gravitational force of Earth pulling down on plate
W_E = gravitational force of plate pulling up on Earth

The two forces are equal, acting to
Newton's third law.

[Total 4 marks]

Mass and Weight

Warm-Up

State whether each of the following statements are true or false.

1) On Earth, the acceleration of an object in free fall is 12 m/s². ...~~false~~... *false*

2) The weight of an object is directly proportional to its mass. ...True...

3) The mass of an object is a measure of the amount of matter in the object. ...True...

1 An astronaut weighs herself on Earth and on the Moon. (Grade 4-6)

a) Explain what is meant by weight.

...Weight is the total amount of matter in an object...

.... *[1]*

b) On Earth, the astronaut has a mass of 65 kg. Calculate her weight on Earth.

$W = m \times g$

$W = 65 \times 10$

6500

Weight = 6500 N
[3]

c) While in space, she wears her spacesuit which has a mass of 80 kg. *80kg*
On the Moon, the astronaut and the spacesuit have a combined weight 232 N.
Calculate the gravitational field strength of the Moon at its surface.

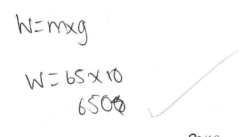

$\dfrac{Weight}{mass}$

$\dfrac{80}{232}$

$(6500 + 232)$

7882

$\dfrac{232}{(80+65)}$

$= 1.6 \, N/kg$

Suit = 80kg
Astronaut = 65 kg

$65 + 80 = 145 kg$

Gravitational field strength = ~~0.34~~ *1.6* .... Unit = ...N./kg.........
[4]

[Total 8 marks]

Exam Practice Tip

When astronauts are in space they experience what we call weightlessness — they do still have a mass, they're just not close enough to a planet or moon to feel its gravitational effect. And remember weight is a force with the unit newtons (N).

Scalars and Vectors

Warm-Up

Write each word below in the table on the right to show whether it is a scalar or vector quantity.

displacement   velocity

speed

distance   force

Scalar	Vector

---

1   Owen kicks a football at a wall. The diagram below shows the path the ball takes after it has been kicked. When it is kicked at point A, the ball moves horizontally to the right until it hits a vertical wall at Point B. The ball then bounces back horizontally to the left and comes to rest at Point C.

A → C = 7

A   v   C   S   B   Scale 1 cm = 1 m

a) Calculate the distance that the ball has moved through from A to B.

Distance = ...7.............. m

[1]

b) Calculate the total distance that the ball has moved through from A to C.

7+5=12

Distance = ...12.............. m

[1]

c) Draw a vector arrow on the diagram above to show the displacement of the ball.

[1]

d) Calculate the magnitude of the displacement of the ball after it has come to rest.

Magnitude of displacement = ... m

[1]

[Total 4 marks]

---

2   Two cars, A and B, start from the same position. They travel at constant speeds in opposite directions. The speed of car A is half the speed of car B.

Choose which row of the table correctly compares the distance travelled, the displacements and the velocities of the cars after 10 seconds.

	Distance travelled	Displacement	Velocity
A	Same	Same	Same
B	Different	Different	Same
C	Different	Different	Different
D	Same	Same	Different

Answer ....

[Total 1 mark]

Chapter P4 — Explaining Motion

Calculating Speed

1 Catherine went for a run. She ran for exactly 22 minutes at an average speed of 4.0 m/s.

a) State the equation relating distance, average speed and time.

$$S = \frac{d}{t}$$

[1]

b) Calculate the distance that Catherine ran in km. Give your answer to **two** significant figures.

$d = S \times t$ Convert into seconds

$22 \times 60 = 1320$

$d = 4 \times 1320$

$= 5.28$

Distance = ~~5.3~~ ~~18.8~~ km

[4]

[Total 5 marks]

2 Cecil is deciding whether to walk or take a bus to get to work. There are two routes he could take. The shorter route is along a 2.8 km path that only pedestrians are allowed to use. The bus takes a longer route along a road.

Cecil is talking to his colleagues about his journey to work.

Cecil
I expect it will take about an hour and a half to walk to work.

a) Estimate how long it would take Cecil to walk the pedestrian route.
Use your answer to determine whether Cecil's expectation is sensible.

$t = \frac{d}{s}$ $d = 2.8 km$ 30×60 ~~3m/s~~ Typical walking speed 1.2 m/s

$\frac{2800}{1.2}$ $= 1800$

$= 2333.\dot{3}$ $\frac{2000}{(60 \times 60)} = 0.\dot{5}$

$= 0.6$ hours

[5]

b) Travelling to work by bus takes 15 minutes. The total distance covered during this time is 7.2 km. Calculate the average speed of the bus in m/s.

$S = \frac{d}{t}$ $t = 15 mins$ $900s$

$d = 7.2$ $7200 m$

$\frac{7200}{900} = 8$

Speed = 8 m/s

[3]

[Total 8 marks]

Chapter P4 — Explaining Motion

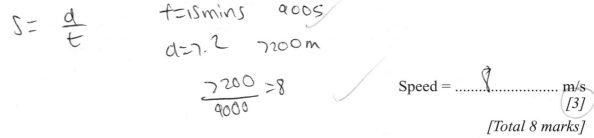

Acceleration

1   Trigger the dog sets off running in a straight line
from rest and reaches a speed of 3.2 m/s in 8.0 s.

$F = m \times a$ $\frac{F}{m/a}$

$\frac{3.2}{8}$

a) Calculate Trigger's acceleration. Give the unit.

Acceleration = ...0.4...... Unit = ...m/s^2...

[4]

b) She keeps running with this acceleration for a further 6.0 s. Calculate Trigger's final speed.

  acceleration = change in speed ÷ time taken

change in speed = acceleration × time taken

0.4 × 60. = 2.4m/s   Speed = ...5.6... m/s

change in speed = final − initial   [3]

final speed = change in speed + initial

c) Trigger continues to run at this final speed in circular loops around the garden.   2.4 + 3.2
Which statement is **correct**?   = 5.6
Place a tick (✓) in the box next to the correct answer.

Trigger is accelerating, but her velocity is constant.   ☐

Trigger is accelerating and her velocity is changing.   ☑

Trigger is not accelerating, but her velocity is constant. ☐

Trigger is not accelerating and her velocity is changing.   ☐

[1]

[Total 8 marks]

2   A boat is travelling across a calm lake. It travels at a constant speed of 5.0 m/s.
It passes a buoy and starts to accelerate with a constant acceleration
of 0.25 m/s^2 until it reaches a second buoy, 1.2 × 10^3 m away.

Calculate the time it takes for the boat to travel between the buoys.

1.2 × 10^3 = 1200

Time = ... s

[Total 5 marks]

Exam Practice Tip

Remember that displacement, velocity and acceleration are all vector quantities, which means they have both a magnitude
and a direction. Whereas distance and speed are scalar quantities, and so they only have a magnitude but no direction.

 ☐   ☐   ☐   Chapter P4 — Explaining Motion

PRACTICAL # Investigating Motion

1   Alice wants to carry out an experiment to investigate the motion of a trolley down a ramp. Her textbook suggests setting up her apparatus as shown in the diagram.

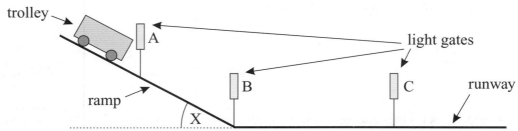

a)* Describe how Alice could use this apparatus to find the acceleration of the trolley down the ramp.

Acceleration = change in speed ÷ time taken.
She can find the time taken from
the trolley to go from A to B. & A to
B and B to C. At the start the initial
speed is 0m/s as the trolley is stationary.

[6]

b) Dana also wants to do the same investigation as Alice, but she can't find any light gates. Dana decides to use a stopwatch instead.

Give **one** disadvantage of using a stopwatch instead of light gates.

Depends on reaction time — might not be accurate.

[1]

c) What would happen to the speed of the trolley on the runway if the angle labelled X in the diagram was increased?

It would decrease increase

[1]

d) The ramp is changed so that its surface is covered with carpet. There is now more friction between the trolley and the ramp. What happens to the speed of the trolley on the runway?

It decreases

[1]

[Total 9 marks]

Distance-Time Graphs

1 A boat is being rowed along a straight canal. Some students time how long after setting off the boat passes marker posts spaced 100 metres apart. The table below shows their results.

Distance (m)	0	100	200	300	400	500
Time (s)	0	85	170	255	340	425

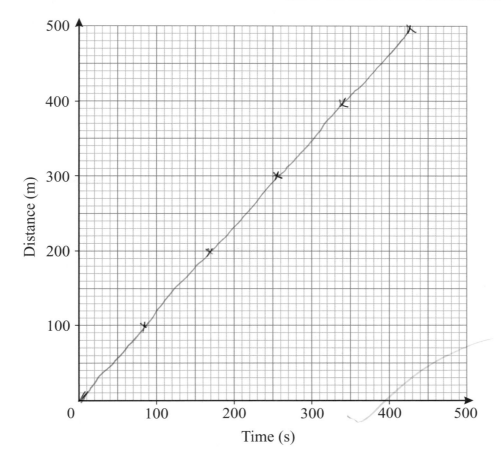

a) Draw the distance-time graph for the results in the table on the grid and axes shown above.

[3]

b) Using the graph, determine how far the boat travelled in 300 s.

Distance = ...350...300...... m

[1]

c) Use the graph to find the time taken for the boat to travel 250 m.

Time = ...210...... s

[1]

d) The students take the timings using a stopwatch. Suggest **one** way the students can make sure their measurements are as accurate as possible.

......Repeat   the   experiment : Referring......
......to the same   point   on the boat......

[1]

[Total 6 marks]

Chapter P4 — Explaining Motion

2 Elena goes for a bike ride. She has a watch that allows her to track how far she has ridden in a given time. When she gets home, she makes a distance-time graph for her journey. The graph she creates is shown to the right.

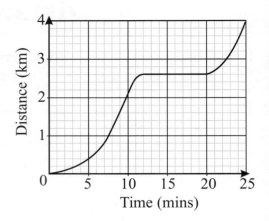

a) Describe Elena's motion during the first ten minutes of her journey.

..........Gradual increase of..................

........distance in 10 mins.................

....

[2]

b) The next day, Elena completes the same route in the same amount of time, but at a constant speed. Calculate Elena's average speed during this time. Give your answer in m/s. Give your answer to **two** significant figures.

$25 \times 60 = 1500$ $4 \times 1000 = 4000$

$\frac{4000}{1500} = 2.66$

Speed ....2.7........ m/s
[4]

[Total 6 marks]

3 The diagram below shows the distance-time graph for a car's journey.

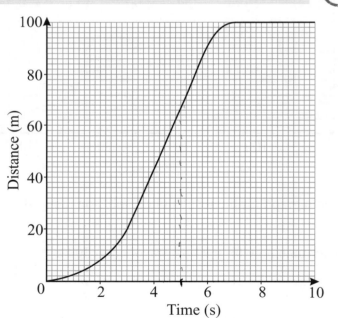

Time (s)

a) Use the graph to find the speed of the car 5 s into its journey.

24

Speed = ...20........... m/s
[3]

b) Use the graph to find the speed of the car 2 s into its journey.

8 m/s

Speed = ... m/s
[3]

[Total 6 marks]

Chapter P4 — Explaining Motion

Velocity-Time Graphs

Use two of the phrases from the list below to correctly label the velocity-time graph.

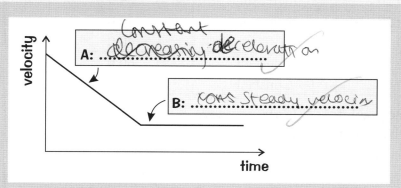

A: ~~decreasing deceleration~~ *constant* deceleration

B: ~~was~~ steady velocity

decreasing deceleration

steady velocity

decreasing acceleration

constant acceleration

constant deceleration

---

1 Velocity-time graphs can be used to show the motion of an object.

Which quantity is represented by the area under a velocity-time graph?
Place a tick (✓) in the box next to the correct answer.

speed ☐

acceleration ☑

distance ☑

deceleration ☐

[Total 1 mark]

---

2 A bear runs with a constant acceleration for 10 s before running at a constant speed
of 8 m/s for a further 10 s. Which of the following speed-time graphs shows this?

A
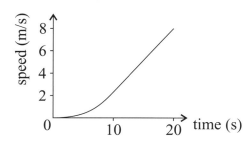

B
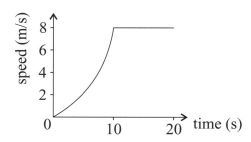

C
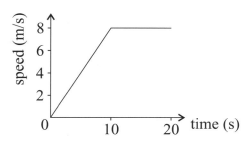

D
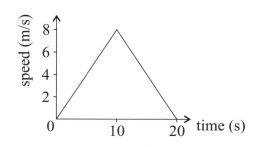

Answer = ...C...

[Total 1 mark]

Chapter P4 — Explaining Motion

3 A lorry is driving along a straight road. The table shows the acceleration of the lorry during different time periods and the lorry's velocity at the end of each time period.

Grade
7-9

Time period (hours)	Acceleration	Final velocity (mph)
0.00 - 0.10	Constant	20.0
0.10 - 0.20	Increasing	24.0
0.20 - 0.30	Increasing	40.0
0.30 - 0.40	0	40.0
0.40 - 0.50	Constant	60.0
0.50 - 0.60	Constant	0.0

a) Complete the velocity-time graph for the lorry's journey.
The first 0.30 hours have been done for you.

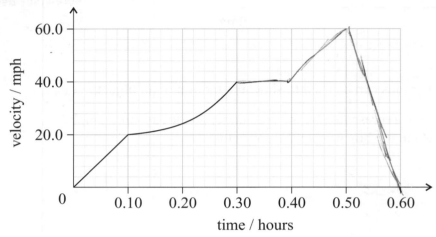

[3]

b) How far does the lorry travel in the first 0.30 hours?

0.02 hours × 4mph = 0.08
0.08 × 78 = 6.24

Distance = ...6.24...... miles
[3]

c) Calculate the acceleration (in m/s²) of the lorry at 0.20 hours. 1 mile = 1600 m.
Give your answer to **two** significant figures.

GiV=82-16+6

2.11 / 720 = 0.0099

Acceleration = ...0.0099... m/s²
[5]

[Total 11 marks]

Exam Practice Tip

A velocity-time graph doesn't just tell you what the velocity of an object is, it can also be used to find the distance travelled by the object and its acceleration throughout its journey. That's a lot of information on one graph.

Chapter P4 — Explaining Motion

Free Body Diagrams and Forces

1 The diagram shows a free body diagram for a truck. The diagram is not to scale.

a) What is the magnitude and direction of the resultant force on the truck?
Place a tick (✓) in the box next to the correct answer.

10 000 N to the left ☐

20 000 N to the left ☑

30 000 N to the right ☐

10 000 N to the right ☑

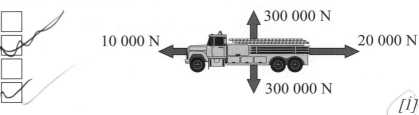

[1]

b) What do we mean by the resultant force acting on an object?

Two or more forces acting at the same time. A resulltant force is the sum of all the individual forces acting on an object taking their directions into account

[2]

c) Name the two 300 000 N forces acting on the truck.

Upwards force = Normal contact force

Downwards force = Gravity Weight

[2]

[Total 5 marks]

2 A child is pushing a heavy box along a carpeted floor.
The box has a weight of 50 N and the child pushes with a
force of 60 N. The overall resultant force on the box is 40 N.

The diagram below is an incomplete free body diagram for the box. The diagram has been drawn to scale. Complete the free body diagram and name the forces acting on the box.

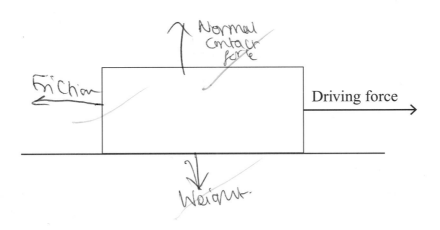

[Total 4 marks]

Exam Practice Tip

Remember — if a free body force diagram has been drawn to scale, both the direction of an arrow and its size are really important. They tell you the direction in which the force represented by the arrow is acting as well as its magnitude.

 ☐ ☐ ☐

Chapter P4 — Explaining Motion

Forces and Scale Drawings

1 Which of the following sentences is **correct** for an object that is in equilibrium? Place a tick (✓) in the box next to the correct answer.

All the forces acting on the object are balanced. ✓

All the forces acting on the object must act in the same direction. ☐

All the forces acting on the object must be the same size. ☐

There is only one force acting on the object. ☐

[Total 1 mark]

2 Which of the following correctly shows the resultant force (solid line) of a horizontal and vertical force (dotted lines) acting on a point?

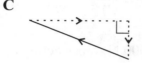

 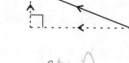

Answer = BxD

[Total 1 mark]

3 A light aircraft is flying north-east in a straight line. The aircraft's engine provides a force of 600 N north. A strong wind is blowing in an easterly direction and provides a force of 800 N on the aircraft.

Draw a scale drawing on the grid below. Find the magnitude of the resultant force on the aircraft.

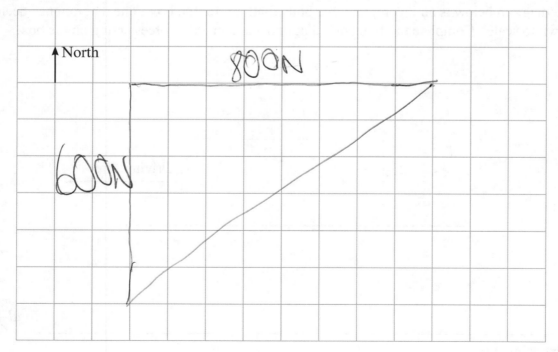

Resultant force = ... N

[Total 3 marks]

Chapter P4 — Explaining Motion

4 Some students, A, B, C and D, are participating in a four-way tug-of-war.
Each rope is pulled by a force acting at 90° to the forces on the ropes on either side.
The diagram below shows an aerial view of the ropes. The forces are drawn to scale.

Scale:
1 cm = 20 N

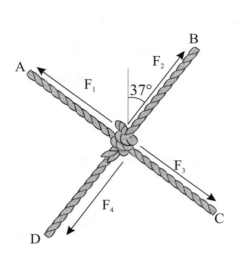

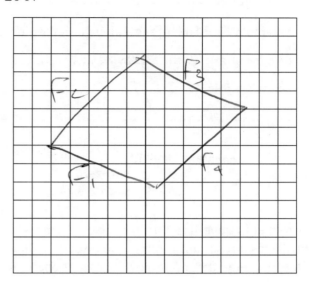

a) By drawing a scale drawing on the grid above, show that the knot at the centre is in equilibrium.

[3]

b) Student A slips, halving the force he applies to the rope.
Student D lets go of his rope entirely.
Using the grid below, use a scale drawing to calculate the size of the resultant force on the knot.

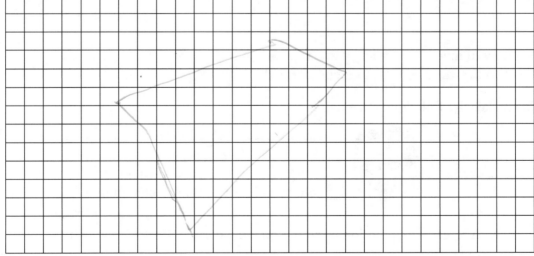

$F = 2.8 \times 20$

56

Resultant force = ... N

[4]

[Total 7 marks]

Chapter P4 — Explaining Motion

64

Newton's First Law and Circular Motion

Use the words below to correctly fill in the gaps in the passage.
You don't have to use every word, but each word can only be used once.

Newton's First Law of motion says that an object will remain stationary

or moving at ...a..... constant velocity.... if the resultant force

acting on it is .... zero .... If the resultant force is

.... non zero ...., it will .... accelerate ....

a constant velocity   accelerate   zero
          non-zero   remain stationary   an increasing speed

1   A rocket is travelling through space. It turns on one of its thrusters, which
    produces a resultant force in the direction shown on the diagram below.
    Describe how the motion of the rocket changes when it experiences this force.

[Grade 4-6]

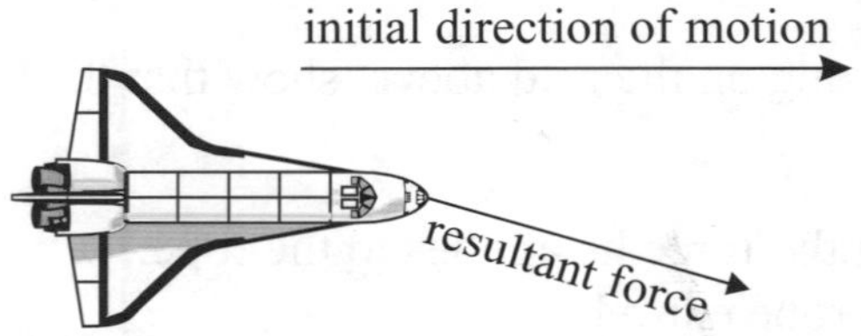

initial direction of motion →

resultant force

..There... would... be... an... increase... in... velocity...........

....

[Total 2 marks]

2   Carlos is swinging a ball attached to a rope around
    his head so that the ball follows a circular path.

[Grade 6-7]

Carlos makes the following statement.

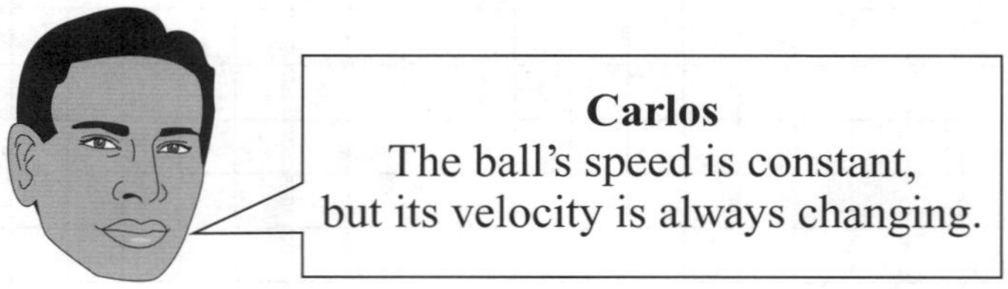

Carlos
The ball's speed is constant,
but its velocity is always changing.

Explain, with reference to the forces acting on the ball, why Carlos' statement is correct.

..The velocity is always changing as there....
..is a constant change in direction........
....
....
....

[Total 3 marks]

Chapter P4 — Explaining Motion

Momentum and Newton's Second Law

1 A vehicle is moving east with a velocity of 15 m/s and momentum 46 000 kg m/s.

Calculate the mass of the vehicle. Give your answer to **two** significant figures.

$P = mv$ $\frac{P}{mv}$

$M = \frac{P}{V}$ $= \frac{46000}{15}$

Mass = ...3066.70......... kg

[Total 4 marks]

2 Sandra is moving some furniture into storage. She fills a trailer and attaches it to her car. She drives north at 20 mph. She then stops and unloads the trailer at a storage depot, which halves the mass of the trailer. She then drives back south at 40 mph.

How will the trailer's momentum have changed compared to when it was travelling north?

	Momentum magnitude	Momentum sign
A	Doubles	Changes from positive to negative
B	No change	Changes from positive to negative
C	Doubles	No change
D	Halves	No change

Answer = ...

[Total 1 mark]

3 Jamie has a Newton's cradle on his desk, like in the diagrams shown below. It consists of five metal balls that all have the same mass, suspended by pieces of thin string.

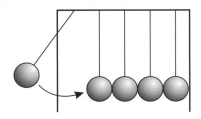 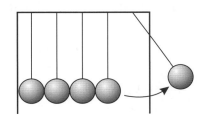

When a ball is lifted and allowed to hit the others as shown in the diagram on the left, it causes the last ball in the line to move outwards, as shown on the right. The balls in between appear to remain stationary. The speed of the first ball when it hits the second ball is equal to the speed of the final ball when it starts to move. Using conservation of momentum, explain this behaviour.

The total momentum before an event is ~~equivat~~ equal to the total momentum after an event.

....

....

....

....

[Total 4 marks]

Chapter P4 — Explaining Motion

4   A stationary red ball with mass m_R is hit by a blue ball with mass $m_B = 4.5 \times 10^{-1}$ kg and velocity $v_B = 3.0$ m/s. The balls collide then move off together at $v_C = 2.5$ m/s.

Before   After

   R   B R

$v_B = 3.0$ m/s $v_{Rc} = 0$ m/s $v_C = 2.5$ m/s
$m_{B_f} = 4.5 \times 10^{-1}$ kg $m_{R_q} = ?$ $m_1 v_1 + m_2 v_2 = m_3 v_3$ $m_C = ?$ tnrs
                                                                          0.5c₁

Calculate the mass of the red ball, m_R.

3 X 0.45   0 + M₂   M = m x V

1.35   +   m₂0   2.5mc

  ₁₃₅ᵏᵍᵐ   1.35 = 2.5mc

              $\frac{1.35 + 225 = mc}{2.5}$

                = -₹ʈ·₅ 0.54

Mr = mc - MB   Mass = ...0.09... kg
   = 0.54 - 0.45   [Total 5 marks]
   = 0.09

5   Ball A has a mass of $m_A = 2.0$ kg. Ball B has a mass of $m_B = 3.0$ kg. Both are moving in the same direction. Ball A is moving faster than ball B, so the two collide. After the collision, both balls move off together in the same direction.

Just before the collision, ball A has a velocity of $v_A = 1.7$ m/s and ball B has a velocity of $v_B = 1.2$ m/s. 3.0 s after the collision, the two balls have a velocity of $v_{A+B} = 0.50$ m/s. Calculate the magnitude of the frictional force acting on the two balls after the collision.

MA = 2.0 kg   MB = 3.0 kg   u   Before   After 3.5
VA = 1.7 m/s   VB = 1.2 m/s   v   V = 0.5 m/s
2 x .7 = 3.4   3 x 1.2 = 3.6   M = 5kg
          3.4 + 3.6
          = 7 kg/m   F = m x a
N = m x V   F = (2+3) x -0.3
$\frac{7}{5}$ 7 = 5 x v   5 x -0.3
$\frac{7}{5}$ = v = 1.4 m/s   = 1.5 N

V = u + a t   0.5 = 1.4 + 3a
V = 0.5   0.5 - 1.4 = 3a
U = 1.4 $\frac{0.5 - 1.4}{3}$ = a = -0.3   Force = ...1.5... N
a = -0.3   [Total 6 marks]
t = 3

Exam Practice Tip

Be careful with collision questions. If two objects are travelling in opposite directions and collide head on, since momentum is a vector, one momentum will be positive and the other will be negative. If the question doesn't tell you which direction is positive, you can choose, but make sure you state clearly which direction you've chosen to be positive in your answer.

😐 ☐   🙂 ☐   😊 ☐

Newton's Second Law and Inertia

1 Suraj decides to investigate how the mass of a shopping trolley affects how easy it is to move.

He takes three identical shopping trolleys, A, B and C, and fills them with different items so that each trolley has a different mass. He pushes each trolley with an equal force from the same starting point, and records the velocity of each immediately afterwards. The table below shows the results.

Trolley	A	B	C
Velocity (m/s)	1.5	0.7	2.2

a) State the meaning of the term inertial mass.

.......*How difficult it is to change the velocity of an object.*.................
[1]

b) State which trolley has the highest inertial mass. Explain your answer.

....

....
[2]

[Total 3 marks]

2 Ball A is rolling freely along a surface. There is a frictional force of 0.50 mN acting on the ball, so that it's decelerating at 0.0025 m/s².

a) Calculate the mass of ball A.

Mass = ... kg
[3]

b) Ball B has the same mass as ball A. It is rolling along a surface where a frictional force of 0.25 mN acts on it. The initial velocity of ball B is the same as the initial velocity of ball A.

Choose the row of the table which correctly compares the change in momentum and time taken for each ball to come to a complete stop.

	Change in momentum of ball B	Time taken for ball B to come to a complete stop
A	the same as ball A	the same as ball A
B	the same as ball A	double that of ball A
C	double that of ball A	the same as ball A
D	double that of ball A	double that of ball A

Answer ....
[1]

[Total 4 marks]

Exam Practice Tip

Newton's three laws of motion are really important. Not only will you need to learn them all, but it's important that you can explain the creativity and imagination which was required to create them. You might be asked to do so in an exam question. Remember, they're expressed in a way which can be easily understood and applied to many different scenarios.

Chapter P4 — Explaining Motion

Moments, Levers and Gears

State whether each of the following statements are true or false.

Gears can only turn clockwise. ......False..........

A lever can produce a large output force from a small input force. ....True..........

1 The diagram below shows several gears that are linked together.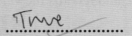

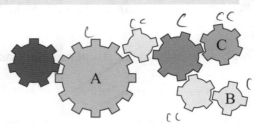

a) If gear A is turned clockwise, in which direction will gears B and C turn?

Gear B: ....Clockwise.......... Gear C: ....anti clockwise..........

[2]

b) Which of the labelled gears will turn the fastest?
Place a tick (✓) in the box next to the correct answer.

Gear A ☑

Gear B ☐

Gear C ☐

They all turn at the same speed. ☐

[1]

[Total 3 marks]

2 Amy is a mechanic. She uses a box spanner to tighten a loose nut. She applies a force of 50 N at the end of the spanner.

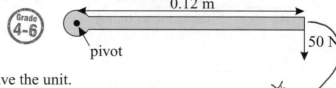

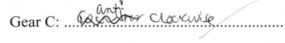

a) Calculate the size of the moment created. Give the unit.

$M = r \times F$ 0.12 × 50

Moment = ...6.......... Unit = ...Nm..........

[3]

b) In which direction will the spanner turn?

..........Clockwise..........

[1]

[Total 4 marks]

3 Two people reach a manual revolving door at the same time.
Each person pushes one wing of the door with a different force and
at a different distance from the pivot, as shown in the diagram below.

Diagram not
to scale.

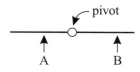

Person A pushes with force of 40 N, 0.5 m from the pivot.
Person B pushes with force of 24 N, 0.7 m from the pivot.

Would the door turn clockwise, anticlockwise or stay as it is (in equilibrium)?
Show your working.

$40 \times 0.5 = 20$

$24 \times 0.7 = 16.8$

Answer = ...Clockwise........

[Total 3 marks]

4 Two children are playing outside. One child, with a weight of 420 N,
stands on one end of a plank of wood as shown in the diagram.
The other child pushes down on the opposite end of the plank of wood.

Diagram not
to scale.

P

2.4 m

0.60 m

What force should the child apply to point P in order to lift the child stood on the plank?

Moment = $p \times d$

42×2.4
$= 100.8$ ✗

420×0.6
$= 252$ Nm

$252 \div 2.4 = 105$ N

Force = ...100.80..... N
[Total 4 marks]

5 Three children are playing on a seesaw. They sit in such a way that the seesaw
is balanced. The diagram below shows the positions and weights of the three
children. Calculate child C's distance from the pivot. Give you answer in metres.

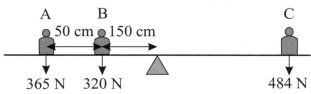

A   B   C
50 cm   150 cm

Diagram not
to scale.

365 N   320 N   484 N

$50 + 150 = 200$
$\frac{200}{100} = 2$
$\frac{150}{100} = 1.5m$

$(365 \times 2) + (320 \times 1.5)$

Distance = ...1.210.......... m
[Total 5 marks]

Chapter P4 — Explaining Motion

Reaction Times

1 A teacher tests the reaction times of two of her students by measuring how far a ruler falls before the student catches it. *Grade 4-6*

a) Describe the steps involved when using the ruler drop experiment to investigate reaction times.

Hold a ruler between the open forefinger and
the thumb of the person being tested.
They drop the ruler and person B has
to start the stopwatch until person A
catches the ruler again.

....

....

[5]

b) The results in the table show the distance the ruler falls during each attempt. Complete the table.

	Attempt 1 (cm)	Attempt 2 (cm)	Attempt 3 (cm)	Average (cm)
Student A	7.0	7.1	6.9	~~16 run~~ 7
Student B	8.4	8.2	8.3	8.3

$(8.3 \times 3) - 8.4 - 8.3 - 8.2$

[2]

c) Which student has the faster reaction time? Give a reason for your answer.

Student A because average falling distance was less than
Student B's.

[1]

[Total 8 marks]

2 Carl tests his reaction time with a metre ruler using a ruler drop experiment. He catches the metre ruler after it has fallen 45.0 cm. Calculate his reaction time. *Grade 7-9*

The acceleration due to gravity is 10 m/s².

(final speed)² − (initial speed)² = 2 × ~~acceleration × distance~~ acceleration × distance.

(final speed)² = 0 + (2 × 10 × 0.45) = 9

final speed = 3 m/s

acceleration = change in speed / time taken

so time taken = change in speed / acceleration = 3/10 = 0.3

Reaction time = ...0.3........ s

[Total 4 marks]

Chapter P4 — Explaining Motion

Stopping Distances

Use the words below to correctly fill in the gaps in the passage.
You don't have to use every word, but each word can only be used once.

The ......*stopping*...... distance of a vehicle is made up of the reaction distance

and the ......*braking*...... distance. The braking distance of a car is ......*longer*......

if the car is heavily loaded and if conditions are ......*icy*...... .

A vehicle is more likely to skid in wet conditions if its tyres are ......*bald*...... .

shallower	shorter	reaction	stopping
braking	icy	bald	
longer	noisy	distracting	deeper

1 The reaction distance for a driver in a car travelling at 40 mph is 12 m. The braking distance is 24 m. *(Grade 4-6)*

a) Calculate the car's stopping distance when it is travelling at 40 mph.

stopping distance = thinking distance + braking distance

= 12 + 24

= 36

Stopping distance = ...36...... m

[1]

b) Give **one** factor that would increase the driver's reaction distance.

......If the speed of the car is higher......

[1]

[Total 2 marks]

2 Motorcyclists wear helmets to protect their heads from injury. *(Grade 6-7)*

a) A motorcycle helmet contains a layer of crushable foam. Explain, in terms of forces and momentum, how this feature helps protect a motorcyclist's head in the event of a crash.

......The soft foam will soften the impact of the crash by reducing any injuries.......

[3]

b) Give **two** safety features of a car which work in the same way as the foam in a motorcycle helmet.

......Air bags......

......Crumple zones......

[2]

[Total 5 marks]

Chapter P4 — Explaining Motion

3 A car is travelling at 30 mph along a road in dry conditions. (Grade 6-7)

a) Which is the best estimate of the car's stopping distance?
Place a tick (✓) in the box next to the correct answer.

2.5×10^2 m ☐   0.1 km ☐

25 m ☐   9 m ☐

[1]

Diane is discussing how the stopping distance of the car varies with speed.

> **Diane**
> If the car doubles its speed,
> the reaction distance will double,
> but the braking distance won't change.

b) Is Diane's statement correct? Explain why.

NO because if you're travelling at a higher speed,
it will takes longer for the car to brake ~~to~~ and
become stationary.

[3]

[Total 4 marks]

4 A car of typical mass is travelling at a speed of 18 m/s.
A deer jumps out in front of the car, so the driver performs an emergency stop.
The brakes of the car exert a force with a magnitude of 6000 N. (Grade 7-9)

a) The work done by the brakes to stop the car is equal to 162 000 J.
Calculate the car's braking distance.

Distance = ... m
[3]

b) The driver's reaction time is 0.5 s. Calculate the overall stopping distance of the car.

Distance = ... m
[2]

c) The driver avoids the deer, and continues on their journey. Later, the car is travelling back when a second deer jumps out in front of it, and the driver performs another emergency stop. The force exerted by the brakes is still 6000 N. Estimate the magnitude of the deceleration of the car.

Magnitude of the deceleration = ... m/s^2
[4]

[Total 9 marks]

Work Done and Energy Transfers

Use the words below to correctly fill in the gaps in the passage.
You don't have to use every word, but each word can only be used once.

If a .... does work on a stationary object, it may cause it to move.

Energy is transferred to its .... energy store.

If there is no .... or air resistance acting on the object,

then the energy transferred will be equal to the ....

force	battery	kinetic	work done	heating
electromagnetic	gravity	weight	friction	acceleration

1 Work done can be measured in joules or newton meters. (Grade 4-6)

Which of the following is equal to 75 kJ?
Place a tick (✓) in the box next to the correct answer.

75 000 Nm ☐

1500 Nm ☐

7.5 Nm ☐

35 Nm ☐

[Total 1 mark]

2 A box is pulled along a frozen pond by an electric winch with a 21.0 N force. The box is dragged 35.0 m to the edge of the pond. You can assume the friction between the box and the ice is negligible. (Grade 6-7)

a) Calculate the work done on the box.

Work done = ... J
[3]

b) The force pulling the box is removed at the edge of the pond. The box then slides onto a paved path, where it slows down to a stop. The average frictional force acting on the box from the path is 17.5 N. Calculate the distance the box travels before stopping.

Distance = ... m
[3]

[Total 6 marks]

Chapter P4 — Explaining Motion

Kinetic and Potential Energy Stores

1 Sarah has a mass of 65 kg and climbs up some stairs from the ground floor of a building to a height of 10 m.

Calculate the amount of energy in Sarah's gravitational potential energy store at the top of the stairs. Use the gravitational field strength = 10 N/kg.

Energy = ... J

[Total 3 marks]

2 Mario collects information about four cars, labelled A-D. All of the cars travel at a steady speed.

a) The masses and speeds of the cars are shown in the table below. Which car has the most energy in its kinetic energy store?

	Mass (kg)	Speed (m/s)
A	1500	11
B	1000	15
C	1800	10
D	2000	8

Answer = ...

[1]

Before reaching a constant speed, Car A was parked partway up a hill. The driver released the handbrake and allowed the car to roll freely down the hill. When the car reached the bottom of the hill, it was travelling at the speed shown in the table above.

b) Calculate the height Car A was parked at. Assume there is no friction or air resistance acting against the car. Give your answer to **two** significant figures. Use the gravitational field strength = 10 N/kg.

Height = ... m

[5]

[Total 6 marks]

Energy Transfers and Power

1   Stephanie buys a light bulb from a shop. It has a power of 60 W.   *Grade 4-6*

Which statement is correct for a 60 W bulb?
Place a tick (✓) in the box next to the correct answer.

It transfers 60 J of energy every second. ☐

It transfers 60 J of energy every 2 seconds. ☐

It transfers 60 J of energy every hour. ☐

It transfers 60 kJ of energy every second. ☐

[Total 1 mark]

2   Jon enjoys playing golf. Describe the energy transfers that occur when a golf club hits a golf ball.   *Grade 6-7*

....

....

....

....

....

[Total 4 marks]

3   A car contains a worn out engine with a power of 32 000 W. The car takes 9.0 s to accelerate from rest to 15 m/s. A mechanic replaces the engine with a more powerful but otherwise identical one. The new engine has a power of 64 000 W.   *Grade 7-9*

a) Explain how the new engine will affect the time it takes for the car to accelerate from rest to 15 m/s.

....

....

....

....

[3]

b) Calculate how long it will take for the car to accelerate to 15 m/s now. You can assume that the total amount of energy wasted whilst the car is accelerating is the same for both engines.

Time = ... s

[4]

[Total 7 marks]

Chapter P5 — Radioactive Materials

Developing the Model of the Atom

1   Our understanding of the structure of the atom has
    changed significantly since the early 19th century.   **Grade 4-6**

a) In 1804, Dalton believed that atoms were tiny spheres which could not be broken up.
    Explain how this theory was disproved by a discovery made by Thomson.

    ....

    ....

    [2]

b) The Rutherford-Geiger-Marsden alpha particle scattering experiment provided evidence for
    the nuclear model of the atom. Describe the model that it replaced.

    ....

    ....

    [1]

c) What did Niels Bohr contribute to the nuclear model of the
    atom in terms of the arrangement of electrons in the atom?

    ....

    ....

    [1]

    [Total 4 marks]

2   Describe the observations made during the Rutherford-Geiger-Marsden alpha particle
    scattering experiment. Explain what these indicated about atomic structure.   **Grade 4-6**

    ....

    ....

    ....

    ....

    ....

    ....

    [Total 4 marks]

Isotopes and Radioactive Decay

The standard notation used to represent atoms is shown. Use the words below to correctly fill in the labels. You don't have to use every phrase, but each phrase can only be used once.

$$^{A}_{Z}X$$

electron number

neutron number

mass number

chemical symbol

charge   atomic number

---

1 Unstable isotopes can emit nuclear radiation, such as alpha particles. **Grade 4-6**

a) Place a tick (✓) in the box that shows what an alpha particle is made up of.

Two neutrons and two protons. ☐

An electron. ☐

A proton and an electron. ☐

Four neutrons and two protons. ☐

[1]

b) Some isotopes will emit an electromagnetic wave as well as an alpha particle. Name the wave.

....

[1]

[Total 2 marks]

---

2 Atom A and atom B are isotopes of an element. The mass number of atom A is 16. Atom A contains 8 neutrons and atom B contains 9 neutrons. **Grade 6-7**

a) Calculate the mass number of atom B.

Mass number = ...

[2]

b) An isotope of neon is $^{23}_{10}$Ne. State whether or not the charge on the neon isotope's nucleus is different to the charge on the nucleus of atom A. Explain your answer.

....

....

....

[2]

[Total 4 marks]

Chapter P5 — Radioactive Materials

Penetration Properties and Decay Equations

1 A beta particle (an electron) is emitted from a nucleus.

   a) State the effect this has on the charge of the nucleus.

....
                                            [1]

   b) After emitting the electron, the atom is excited. The atom releases its excess energy in the form of a gamma ray. Describe what effect, if any, this has on the charge and mass of the nucleus.

....
                                            [1]

                                           [Total 2 marks]

2 Anandi carries out an experiment to investigate two different radioactive sources, Source A and Source B. Each radioactive source emits only one type of radiation. A setup of her experiment is shown below. Each time the radiation from a radioactive decay reaches the radiation detector, it records a 'count'. Anandi changes the material between the source and the radiation detector and measures the count rate — the number of counts recorded every minute. A table of her results is also shown.

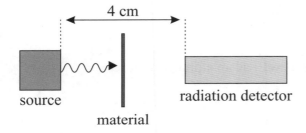

Material	Count rate (counts per minute)	
	Source A	Source B
No material	1203	854
Paper	7	851
Aluminium	6	8
Lead	6	7

   a) What happens to the mass number and charge of the nuclei of source A when they decay?

....

....
                                            [2]

   b) Source B is an isotope of carbon (C), which has a mass number of 14 and an atomic number of 6. The carbon nuclei decay to nitrogen (N) nuclei. Write a balanced equation to show this decay.

....
                                            [4]

   c) State which source emits the radiation that has the longest range in air.

....
                                            [1]

                                           [Total 7 marks]

Exam Practice Tip

You need to know how the penetration properties of alpha, beta and gamma radiation differ. For example, gamma radiation has the longest range in air and alpha radiation has the shortest. Beta radiation sits somewhere in between.

Activity and Half-life

1   Fin wants to find the half-life of a radioactive sample in his lab. He carries out
    an experiment using the sample and produces the graph below from his results.
    The graph shows how the activity of the radioactive sample changed over time.

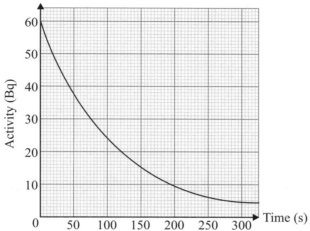

a) Define the term 'half-life' in terms of activity.

    ....
                                                                                                        [1]

b) Using the graph above, determine the half-life of the sample.

                                                    Half-life = ... s
                                                                                                        [1]

c) Initially, the sample contained approximately 800 undecayed nuclei.
    Predict how many of these nuclei will have decayed after two half-lives.

                                                    Decayed nuclei = ...
                                                                                                        [2]

d) Place a tick (✔) in the box that shows the fraction of
    nuclei that remain undecayed after two half-lives.

    $\frac{1}{2}$ ☐ $\frac{2}{1}$ ☐ $\frac{1}{4}$ ☐ $\frac{4}{1}$ ☐
                                                                                                        [1]
                                                                                            [Total 5 marks]

2   The table shows data about two radioactive sources.

	Isotope 1	Isotope 2
Number of undecayed nuclei	20 000	20 000
Half-life	4 minutes	72 years

Explain which isotope will have the highest activity initially.

    ....

    ....
                                                                                                        [Total 1 mark]

Chapter P5 — Radioactive Materials

80

3 Sam is using a radioactive sample with a 50 second half-life in his experiment. The initial activity of the sample is 120 Bq.

a) Complete the graph below to show how the activity of the sample will change in the first 160 s.

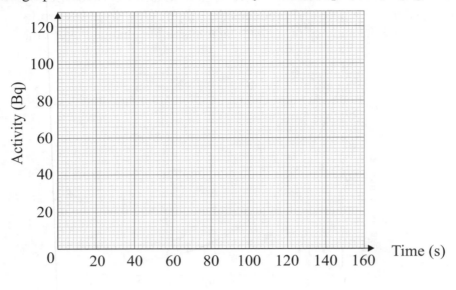

[3]

b) Use your graph to predict the activity of the sample after 40 s.

Activity = ... Bq

[1]

[Total 4 marks]

4 The activity of a radioisotope is 8800 Bq. After 1 hour and 15 minutes, the activity has fallen to 6222 Bq. A further 1 hour and 15 minutes after that, the activity has fallen to 4400 Bq.

a) Calculate the radioisotope's half-life. Give your answer in **minutes**.

Half-life = ... minutes

[2]

b) Calculate the activity of the isotope after a total time of 6 hours and 15 minutes has passed. Give your answer to **two** significant figures.

Activity = ... Bq

[3]

[Total 5 marks]

Exam Practice Tip

Half-life and activity are really important things to get your head around — they're a key thing to mention when talking about any radioactive substance. Remember that every activity-time graph showing radioactive decay has the same shape — radioactive decay is a random process, but by looking at lots of nuclei you can make fairly accurate estimates.

Chapter P5 — Radioactive Materials

Dangers of Radioactivity

For each statement, tick whether it is true or false.

	True	False
Contamination and irradiation only last as long as the original source is present.	☐	☐
Contamination is temporary, but irradiation lasts longer.	☐	☐
Irradiation is temporary, but contamination lasts longer.	☐	☐
Contamination and irradiation continue after the original source has been removed.	☐	☐

1 Rebekah is looking at three samples of different radioactive sources they use in her lab. Each sample contains approximately the same number of radioactive nuclei and have similar initial activities and half-lives. A table showing the properties of the sources is given.

Grade 6-7

Source	Radiation Emitted	Form
A	Alpha	Solid
B	Alpha and gamma	Gas
C	Gamma	Gas

a) Which source poses the greatest risk to those using it? Explain your answer.

....

....

....

....

[3]

Rebekah writes out some safe handling instructions for the lab.

Safety precautions for working with radioactive sources

- Always wear gloves when working with radioactive sources.
- Keep sources as close to you as possible at all times.
- Use tongs to handle any solid radioactive material.
- Place sources in a lead lined box when not in use.

She has made **one** mistake.

b) Circle the incorrect statement. Explain why this statement is incorrect.

....

....

....

[2]

[Total 5 marks]

Chapter P5 — Radioactive Materials

Half-life and Uses of Radiation

1   The table below outlines some properties of four radioactive materials. One of the materials is used in a medical procedure to trace the blood flow to the heart in order to detect blockages within the arteries.

Which is the best source to use in this procedure?

	Type of radiation emitted	Half-life
A	Gamma	6 hours
B	Beta	500 years
C	Alpha	4 hours
D	Gamma	70 years

Answer ....
[Total 1 mark]

2   Ewan is comparing two sources, X and Y. X and Y emit the same type of radiation and initially have the same number of radioactive nuclei. Source X has a half-life of 24 hours and source Y has a half-life of 10 years.

Ewan makes the following statement:

Ewan
It is initially safer to be around source X than source Y.

Is Ewan's statement true or false? Explain your answer.

....

....
[Total 1 mark]

3   A patient is receiving cancer treatment. They undergo a procedure to have a beta-emitting implant placed next to their tumour. In a few months, they will have the implant removed.

a) Explain why a beta-emitting source is used for the implant.

....

....

....
[2]

b) Why will the implant be removed after a few months?

....

....
[1]
[Total 3 marks]

4* A tumour in the body can be treated using an external gamma radiation source. Explain why gamma radiation is used and the process involved. You should include any steps taken to protect healthy cells in your answer.

Grade 6-7

....

....

....

....

....

....

....

....

....

....

[Total 6 marks]

5 Sources of radiation can be used in medical imaging to explore internal organs. Iodine-123 is a radioactive isotope that is absorbed by the thyroid. Grave's disease causes an overactive thyroid, so the thyroid will absorb more iodine than usual.

Grade 7-9

a) Briefly explain how iodine-123 could be used to determine if a patient has Grave's disease.

....

....

....

....

....

[3]

b) Iodine-123 emits gamma radiation. Give **two** reasons why an alpha emitter wouldn't be used for determining if a patient has Grave's disease.

....

....

[2]

[Total 5 marks]

Exam Practice Tip

Ionising radiation can cause cells to mutate and divide uncontrollably. But it can also be used to kill cancerous cells. You need to understand how this is done with radiotherapy, including why different types of radiation are used.

Chapter P5 — Radioactive Materials

Fission and Fusion

For the sentences below, state whether they are describing nuclear fission, nuclear fusion or both.

It releases energy, which is carried away by radiation. ....

Is used to generate energy in nuclear power stations. ....

It usually involves large and unstable nuclei. ....

It usually involves light nuclei. ....

1   Nuclear fusion is the process by which stars generate energy.
Alpha Centauri A is a star which contains hydrogen.

Grade 4-6

Use phrases from the box below to complete the passage.
You can only use a phrase **once** and you do not need to use all the phrases.

electrons	helium nuclei	charge	mass	hydrogen nuclei

In Alpha Centauri A, ... can fuse together

to form .... During nuclear fusion, some of the

.... is converted into energy.

[Total 3 marks]

2   The plutonium isotope $^{239}_{94}$Pu can undergo fission when
it absorbs a neutron, to produce two daughter nuclei.

Grade 6-7

a) Which row of the table shows the most likely number
of protons and neutrons in the daughter nuclei?

	Daughter nucleus 1		Daughter nucleus 2	
	Number of protons	Number of neutrons	Number of protons	Number of neutrons
A	54	80	40	63
B	91	140	3	3
C	89	138	5	5
D	7	7	87	136

Answer ....
[1]

b) Give **one** reason for your answer to part a).

....

....
[1]

[Total 2 marks]

Density

1 Sayid is investigating the properties of two objects he has in his lab. The two objects are made of different materials and are shown below, along with some of their properties.

Object A

Object B

area = 0.050 m²

length = 0.40 m

mass = 1.60 kg
volume = 0.02 m³

density of material = 950 kg/m³

a) Write down the equation that links density, mass and volume.

....

[1]

b) Calculate the density of object A.

Density = ... kg/m³
[2]

c) Calculate the mass and volume of object B.

Volume = ... m³

Mass = ... kg
[3]

[Total 6 marks]

PRACTICAL

2 Alexis has some rings. She wants to find out what materials they're made from. She uses the apparatus shown below to calculate the volumes of three different rings.

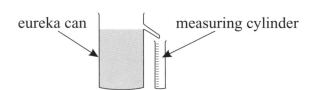
eureka can   measuring cylinder

The eureka can is filled up to the spout so that when a ring is placed in the can, the displaced water flows into the measuring cylinder. Her results are shown in the table on the next page.

She knows that one ring is made from gold, one is made from silver and the other is made from titanium. Complete the table on the next page using the following information:
Density of gold = 19 g/cm³   Density of silver = 10 g/cm³   Density of titanium = 4.5 g/cm³

Ring	Mass (g)	Water displaced (ml)	Material
A	5.7	0.30	....
B	2.7	0.60	....
C	3.0	0.30	....

[Total 5 marks]

PRACTICAL

3* The diagram on the right shows a density bottle.
When full, the density bottle holds exactly 100 ml of any liquid.

A student is given a density bottle, a mass balance and a liquid of known density.
Describe how the student could use this equipment to calculate the density
of a small, irregularly-shaped object.

....

....

....

....

....

....

....

....

....

....

....

....

....

....

[Total 6 marks]

Exam Practice Tip

You may be asked about experiments you've never seen before in an exam, but don't panic. Take your time to read all the information carefully, link it to what you do know and work out what's going on before attempting any questions.

Chapter P6 — Matter — Models and Explanations

The Particle Model

The images below show the particles in a substance when it is in three different states of matter.
Label each image to show whether the substance is a solid, a liquid or a gas.

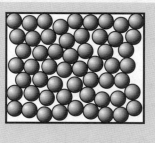 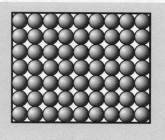 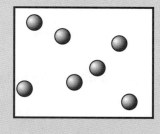

....

1   Use words from the box below to complete the passage.
You can only use a word **once** and you do not need to use all the words.

mass	increases	temperature	decreases

When a system is heated, the internal energy of the system ....

This either increases the .... of the system or causes a change of state.

[Total 2 marks]

2   Harvey accidentally leaves a tub of ice cream out of the freezer. By the time he realises,
the ice cream has melted. He places the ice cream back in the freezer to freeze it.

a)   Melting and freezing are both changes of state. Give the name of the following changes of state:

Gas to liquid: ....   Liquid to gas: ....

[1]

b)   The ice cream undergoes a physical change when it melts.
State what is meant by the term 'physical change'.

....

....

[1]

c)   When the ice cream changes state, the density of the ice cream also changes.
Place a tick (✓) in the box that is a **true** statement about the different states of matter.

A liquid is usually less dense than a gas.   ☐

A liquid is usually more dense than a solid.   ☐

A solid is usually more dense than a gas.   ☐

A solid is usually less dense than a gas.   ☐

[1]

[Total 3 marks]

3 A bicycle has a flat tyre. Pamela pumps up the tyre until it is at its maximum volume. (Grade 6-7)

a) Explain what would happen to the tyre pressure if Pamela pumped more air into the tyre, but the volume of the tyre remained the same.

....

....

....

[3]

b) Pamela makes the following statement:

> **Pamela**
> If the tyre stays at a constant volume, the tyre pressure will be higher on a hot day compared to a cold day.

Is Pamela correct? Explain your answer.

....

....

....

....

[3]

[Total 6 marks]

4 Cassie adds ice to her glass of water. She notices that the ice cubes float. (Grade 6-7)

a) The ice cubes float because ice is less dense than liquid water. Explain what this suggests about the arrangement of the water molecules in each state.

....

....

....

[2]

b) Explain what happens to the total mass of the glass and its contents as the ice melts.

....

....

....

[2]

[Total 4 marks]

Exam Practice Tip

The particle model is widely used to explain the behaviour of substances in different states. Make sure you can explain observed behaviour in terms of the motion and energies of the particles that make up a substance.

Chapter P6 — Matter — Models and Explanations

Specific Heat Capacity

The snippets below show the parts of the definition of specific heat capacity.
Number each snippet 1 to 6 to show the correct order. The first one has been done for you.

☐1 The specific heat capacity of a substance is...

☐ ...of 1 kg of the substance...

☐ ...by 1 °C.

☐ ...the energy required...

☐ ...to increase...

☐ ...the temperature...

PRACTICAL

1* A student carries out an experiment to find the specific heat capacity of aluminium. Grade 4-6

The diagram shows the setup the student uses in her experiment. Describe how the student should carry out the experiment, including how she should calculate the specific heat capacity and make her results more accurate.

electric heater

aluminium cylinder

thermometer

joulemeter

cup packed with cotton wool

....

....

....

....

....

....

....

....

....

[Total 6 marks]

2 1.2 kg of water is heated in a sealed pan. The specific heat capacity of water is 4200 J/kg°C. Grade 6-7

Before heating, the water is at 24 °C. 302 400 J of energy is transferred to the water.
Calculate the temperature of the water after it has been heated.

Temperature = ... °C

[Total 3 marks]

Chapter P6 — Matter — Models and Explanations

Specific Latent Heat

1 An immersion heater is used to boil 0.50 kg of water in a sealed container. **Grade 6-7**

a) Define the term 'specific latent heat'.

....

....

[1]

b) The lid is removed when the water begins to boil. The immersion heater transfers 1.13 MJ of
energy to evaporate all of the water. Calculate the specific latent heat of vaporisation of water.

Specific latent heat = ... MJ/kg

[3]

[Total 4 marks]

2 Fatima is a chemist who is investigating the properties of bromine. **Grade 6-7**

Fatima heats a small sample of frozen bromine in a flask.
The flask is attached to a condenser, which is used to
collect and condense any bromine that evaporates.

The graph on the right shows how the temperature
changes with time as the bromine is heated.

a) Explain why the graph has a flat section during the
time period between 3 minutes and 8 minutes from
the beginning of heating. Using the particle model,
explain what is happening to the bromine during this time.

....

....

....

....

....

[3]

b) Using the graph, give the melting and boiling points of bromine to the nearest °C.

Melting point = ... °C   Boiling point = ... °C

[2]

[Total 5 marks]

Chapter P6 — Matter — Models and Explanations

Pressure

1 Steven is playing with a water cannon on a hot day. Water in the chamber of the cannon is squeezed out when a force is applied by the plunger. A force of 12 N is applied by the plunger. The plunger has a surface area of 0.15 m².

Calculate the pressure exerted by the plunger.

Pressure = ... Pa

[Total 3 marks]

2 Chloe wants to investigate how temperature affects pressure. She sets up the apparatus shown on the right.

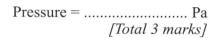

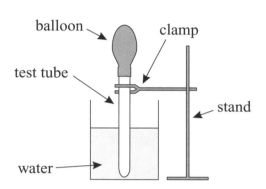

The open end of a test tube is covered with a deflated balloon. No air can get in or out of the test tube or balloon.

The test tube is put into a beaker of 80 °C water.

Chloe observes that as the test tube warms up, the balloon begins to inflate. She knows that the hot water surrounding the test tube is causing the pressure of the air inside the test tube and balloon to increase. She makes the following statement:

> **Chloe**
> The increase in pressure of the air in the test tube causes the balloon to inflate.

State whether or not Chloe's statement is correct. Explain your answer.

....

....

....

....

....

....

....

[Total 3 marks]

Chapter P6 — Matter — Models and Explanations

3 Logan fills a cylinder with helium gas and seals it with an air-tight piston, as shown on the right. The helium is at a pressure of 1.1×10^5 Pa and temperature 24 °C.

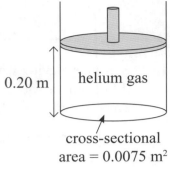

0.20 m | helium gas

cross-sectional area = 0.0075 m²

a) The helium is kept at a constant temperature and the piston is moved upwards. The volume of the helium gas is now 2.75×10^{-3} m³ and its temperature is still 24 °C. Calculate the new pressure of the helium.

Pressure = ... Pa

[4]

b) Logan turns the cylinder on its side before releasing the piston. The piston moves back down the cylinder until it reaches an equilibrium position. Explain why this occurs.

....

....

....

....

....

[3]

[Total 7 marks]

4* The pistons in a diesel engine work by compressing air very quickly and then spraying in droplets of diesel fuel, which then ignites. Explain how compressing the air increases its temperature until it is hot enough to ignite the diesel fuel.

....

....

....

....

....

....

....

....

....

[Total 6 marks]

Exam Practice Tip

Just make sure you know how to work with standard form on your calculator, and practise doing so. And remember, it's not scary, it's just a short-hand way of writing long numbers. For example, $1.1 \times 10^5 = 110\ 000$.

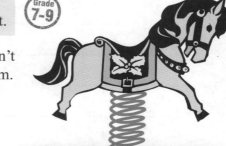

[2]

Chapter P6 — Matter — Models and Explanations

93

Atmospheric Pressure and Liquid Pressure

1 Freya is measuring the pressure at different depths in an unknown liquid. At a depth of 15 cm, the pressure due to the liquid is 2850 Pa. Calculate the density of the liquid.

Grade 4-6

Density = ... kg/m³

[Total 3 marks]

2 Jeff notices that when he goes swimming he feels lighter. He decides to test how the apparent weight of an object changes when it is immersed in water.

Grade 6-7

He attaches a golf ball to a digital force gauge. He uses this to measure the weight of the ball in air and when the ball is lowered into water, as shown in the diagram.

force gauge
0.45 N
0.30 N
golf ball
water

Explain why the weight of the golf ball appears to change when it is placed in the water.

....

....

....

....

[Total 3 marks]

3* Explain what causes atmospheric pressure, and why it decreases with altitude.

Grade 7-9

....

....

....

....

....

....

....

....

....

[Total 6 marks]

Chapter P6 — Matter — Models and Explanations

Forces and Elasticity

Draw a ring around the graph below which shows the force-extension graph of a rubber band.

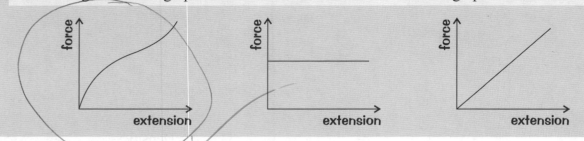

1   Deformations can be elastic or inelastic. Grade 4-6

Explain what is meant by the terms elastic deformation and inelastic deformation.

Elastic deformation is a temporary shape change that is self-reversing after the force is removed. Inelastic deformation is when a material is deformed so much it can't go back to its original state.

[Total 2 marks]

2   A student investigates the change in height of a toy horse in a playground, shown on the right, when different people sit on it. Grade 7-9

a)   When a child weighing 250 N sits on the toy horse his feet don't touch the floor. The height of the toy horse decreases by 20 cm. Calculate the spring constant of the spring. Give the correct unit.

$F = kx$

$k = \dfrac{250}{20}$
0.2
$= 12.5$
$= 1250$

1250

Spring constant = ...12.5...... Unit = ...n/m......
[5]

b)   The child gets off and the student's teacher sits on the toy horse. She lifts her feet so they do not touch the ground. Her weight is double that of the child. The student predicts that the height of the toy horse will change by 40 cm. Explain whether or not you agree with the student. State any assumptions you have made.

I think that I would agree because if the teacher is double the weight then the height of the horse will decrease by 40 cm.

[2]

[Total 7 marks]

Investigating Hooke's Law

1   Eric carried out an investigation to study the relationship between the force exerted on and the extension of a spring. He hung increasing numbers of 1 N weights from the bottom of the spring and measured the extension of the spring with a ruler, as shown below.

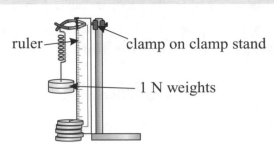

ruler →
← clamp on clamp stand
— 1 N weights

Force (N)	Extension (cm)
0	0.0
1	4.0
2	8.0
3	12.0
4	15.9
5	21.6
6	30.0

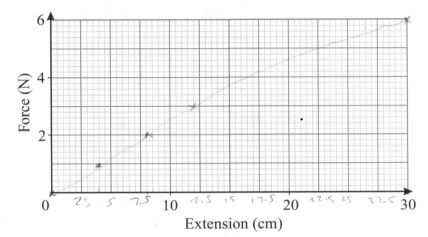

a) The table above shows the results that Eric obtained in his investigation.
    Draw the force-extension graph for Eric's results on the grid and axes above.

[3]

b) Using the graph you have drawn, calculate the spring constant of the spring being tested.

Spring constant = ... N/m

[3]

[Total 6 marks]

2   Calculate the work done on a spring when it is extended elastically by 6.0 cm. The spring constant of the spring is 50 N/m.

W = F×s
   50×6.0
      = 300

Work done = ...300....... J

[Total 3 marks]

Chapter P6 — Matter — Models and Explanations

The Solar System and Orbits

Circle the correct words or phrases below so that the sentences are correct.

The force acting on a planet in orbit acts (towards / away from) the centre of the orbit.

This force is always (parallel / opposite / perpendicular) to the direction of motion of the planet.

This means that the (speed / direction / mass) of the planet constantly changes, while its (velocity / speed / momentum) remains constant.

1 Different objects in our solar system have different orbits. Grade 4-6

a) Complete the table below to show what each type of object orbits around.

Object	Orbits around...
minor planet	Sun
moon	Planet

[2]

b) Name the force that causes a moon's orbit.

Gravitation Gravitational Force Gravity

[1]

c) Artificial satellites are another type of object in our solar system. State **one** similarity and **one** difference between an artificial satellite and a moon in our solar system.

They both orbit circle around planets. One has been made by humans, the other is natural.

[2]

[Total 5 marks]

2 Jupiter is the largest planet in our solar system. It has several moons orbiting it in stable orbits. Niamh is researching two of Jupiter's moons — Io and Callisto. Grade 7-9

Callisto has an average orbital radius of 1 800 000 km.
Io has an average orbital radius of 421 700 km.

Niamh assumes that the moons travel in circular orbits around Jupiter, as shown in the diagram.

Which moon is travelling faster? Explain your answer.

IO because it's much closer to Jupiter meaning it has a stronger gravitational force. The stronger the gravitational force, the quicker you need to travel to stay in a stable orbit.

[Total 3 marks]

The Formation of the Solar System

1 Our Sun is fuelled by a process known as nuclear fusion. (Grade 4-6)

a) Use the correct words from the box to complete the following passage on nuclear fusion in the Sun.

volume	temperature	hydrogen	fission
compressed	fusion	expanded	iron

During the formation of the Sun, a gas cloud was ...*compressed*... and

its ...*temperature*... increased. When the temperature was hot enough,

...*hydrogen*... nuclei underwent nuclear ...*fission*... .

[3]

b) Our Sun is currently in the stable 'main sequence' stage of its lifetime.
Explain how nuclear fusion keeps a star stable at this stage.

The outward pressure/expansion due to nuclear fusion balances the inwards force due to gravitational attraction.

[2]

[Total 5 marks]

2 The solar system was formed when a large cloud of dust and gas collapsed in on itself due to gravity. (Grade 6-7)

a) Explain, in terms of energy transfer and the particle model, how the temperature of the cloud changed as it was compressed.

As the gas cloud was compressed it turned into a solid as all the particles became packed. As the cloud collapsed work was done by gravity to compress the dust and gas. This transferred energy to the kinetic energy stores of the particles which caused an increase in temperature

[3]

b) Describe how the planets were formed from the cloud of dust and gas.

Areas of high density away from the centre of the cloud got denser and hotter and were compressed together to form planets

[2]

[Total 5 marks]

Exam Practice Tip

This is one of those bits of physics where there are just a lot of words and facts to learn. You need to remember the different stages leading up to the formation of the Sun, as well as the processes that keep the Sun stable.

Chapter P6 — Matter — Models and Explanations

Red-Shift and the Big Bang

1   The table below shows a list of galaxies and their distances from Earth in light years.

Galaxy	Distance From Earth (light years)
Cigar Galaxy	12 million
Black Eye Galaxy	24 million
Sunflower Galaxy	37 million
Tadpole Galaxy	420 million

The light from the galaxies in the table shows red-shift.

a) i) Describe what is meant by red-shift.

The space between the Earth and other galaxies are expanding meaning the light waves that reach us would be shifting to the red end of the spectrum.

[2]

ii) From which galaxy in the table will light show the greatest red-shift?
Explain your answer.

Tadpole Galaxy as it has the highest distance. It's travelling away the fastest

[3]

b) Explain how the red-shift of light from distant
galaxies provides evidence for the Big Bang model.

Measurements of red-shift show all the distant galaxies are moving away from us. The more distant a galaxy, the faster it's moving away from us. This support the Universe is expanding

[4]

[Total 9 marks]

Exam Practice Tip

The Big Bang theory is the leading theory of the creation of the Universe — but it wasn't always. In the exam, you might be asked to describe how theories become widely accepted, and how developments in technology can play a part in this. So be prepared to think about the scientific practices that lead us to conclusions about how the Universe works.

Mixed Questions

1 Abbie is walking her dog. She records the distance she has travelled during the walk every 5 minutes.

a) After exactly 5 minutes, she has walked a distance of 420 m.
Calculate the average speed at which she walked during these 5 minutes.
Use the equation:

$$\text{average speed} = \text{distance} \div \text{time}$$

Average speed = ... m/s
[3]

b) She uses the information she collects to draw a distance-time graph for her walk.
What does the gradient of her distance-time graph represent?
Place a tick (✓) in the box next to the correct answer.

her speed ☐   her distance travelled ☐

her acceleration ☐   her deceleration ☐
[1]

c) Whilst walking, the girl throws a ball for her dog to chase.
Each time she throws the ball, she transfers energy to the ball's kinetic energy store.

Which method correctly describes how energy is transferred to the ball?
Place a tick (✓) in the box next to the correct answer.

electrically ☐   by heating ☐

mechanically ☐   by radiation ☐
[1]
[Total 5 marks]

2 All magnets, including permanent and induced magnets, have a north and a south pole. (Grade 4-6)

a) Describe the difference between a permanent magnet and an induced magnet.

....

....
[2]

b) Two permanent magnets are placed with their north poles near to each other.
Which of the following options describes the force exerted by one magnet on the other?
Place a tick (✓) in the box next to the correct answer.

It is an attractive, contact force.   ☐

It is an attractive, non-contact force.   ☐

It is a repulsive, contact force.   ☐

It is a repulsive, non-contact force.   ☐
[1]
[Total 3 marks]

3 Jaden is investigating diodes. (Grade 4-6)

a) Which of the following is the correct circuit symbol for a diode?

    A   **B**   **C**   **D**

Answer = ...
[1]

b) Jaden carries out an experiment in order to plot the *I-V* characteristic of a diode. His graph is shown to the right. Using this graph, explain why you must be careful to connect a diode the correct way round in a circuit.

....

....

....

....

....

[3]

[Total 4 marks]

4 Aureli works for a company that tests the safety features of different vehicles. (Grade 4-6)

Aureli crash tests a car. Initially, the car has a momentum of 18 000 kg m/s. After the collision, the car has a momentum of 0 kg m/s. It takes 0.02 seconds for the car to come to rest.

a) Calculate the resultant force acting on the car during the collision. Use the equation:

change of momentum = resultant force × time for which it acts

Resultant force = ... N
[3]

b) i) State the equation that links force, mass and acceleration.

....

[1]

ii) Aureli performs an emergency stop in a second car to test its brakes.
The car has a mass of 1200 kg. To stop the car, the brakes exert a constant force of −4200 N.
Calculate the deceleration of the car.

Deceleration = ... m/s²
[3]

[Total 7 marks]

Mixed Questions

5 The diagram shows the magnetic field lines around a current-carrying wire.

magnetic field lines — wire

X•

•Y

direction of current •Z

a) At which point in the diagram, X, Y or Z, is the magnetic field weakest?

....

[1]

b) The wire is connected in series with a 12.0 V power supply.
A current of 3.20 A flows through the wire. Calculate the resistance of the wire.

Resistance = ... Ω
[3]
[Total 4 marks]

6 Sam is using a radiation detector to investigate a radioactive source, A.
The radiation detector can be used to measure of the activity of a source.

a) When Sam first measures the activity of source A, it is 7640 Bq.
When he measures it again exactly 16 days later, it has dropped to 1910 Bq.
Find the half-life of the source. Give your answer in **days**.

Half-life = ... days
[2]

b) Sam puts source A in a sealed box lined with a thin layer of lead. When he places the
radiation detector near the box, the detector still detects radiation from the source.
Sam and his friend Maxine both suggest what type of radiation is being detected from source A:

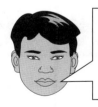

| **Sam** |
| The detector is detecting |
| gamma rays from source A. |

| **Maxine** |
| The detector is detecting |
| alpha particles from source A. |

State whether Sam or Maxine is correct. Explain your answer.

....

....

....

[2]
[Total 4 marks]

7   Romeo is playing with a remote-controlled toy car. The car is powered by a battery. Romeo drives the car in a straight line at its maximum speed.

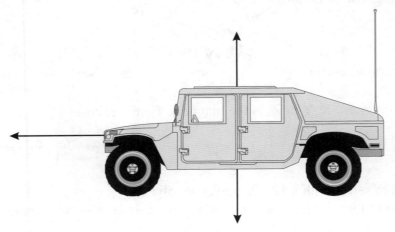

a) The diagram above shows an incomplete force diagram for
    the toy as it travels at its maximum speed.

    Complete the force diagram to show the resultant resistive force acting on the car.

    [2]

b) The car's wheels are powered by a basic electric motor. The efficiency of the motor is 65%.
    During a short journey, a total of 1200 J of energy was transferred to the motor.

    State the equation that links efficiency, the useful energy transferred
    and the total energy transferred.

    ....
    [1]

c) Calculate the useful energy transferred by the motor during the journey.

    Useful energy transferred = ... J
    [3]

d) Describe the energy transfers that take place as the car is driven at its maximum speed.

    ....
    ....
    ....
    ....
    ....
    ....
    [5]
    [Total 11 marks]

8   A bottle of water is placed in the freezer. There is 200 g of water in the bottle and both the water and the bottle are initially at 20 °C. The latent heat of fusion for ice is 330 000 J/kg and the specific heat capacity of water is 4200 J/kg°C.

Calculate the minimum energy that must be transferred from the water so that it completely freezes. Give your answer to **two** significant figures.

Energy transferred = ... J

[Total 5 marks]

9   An astronomer is studying stars in a nearby galaxy.

He collects data about the radiation emitted by the stars. The diagram below shows a plot of the wavelengths of radiation emitted by two of the stars, and the intensity of each emitted wavelength.

Key

Star A	- - - - - -
Star B	————

a)   State if the surface temperature of star B is higher or lower than that of star A. Explain your answer.

....

....

....

[2]

b)   The astronomer is using a telescope mounted on a satellite. Satellite-mounted telescopes were a development in telescope technology that greatly improved the quality of data that could be collected. Suggest **one** other way telescope technology has developed over time. Explain how this development has affected the information available to scientists.

....

....

....

....

[2]

[Total 4 marks]

Mixed Questions

10 Helene is investigating how the deceleration of a 0.50 kg trolley varies based on the surface it is travelling on. Her set-up is shown below.

Helene uses a spring attached to the wall to provide the driving force for the trolley. For each repeat she pushes the trolley against the spring until the spring is compressed by 0.040 m, then releases it and measures its speed at each light gate.

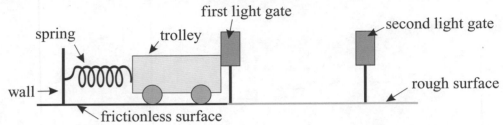

a) State **one** independent variable and **one** dependent variable.

Independent variable: ....

Dependent variable: ....

[2]

b) i) After the spring is released, the first light gate records the trolley's speed just after it leaves the spring. Its speed is found to be 0.60 m/s. You can assume that no friction acts upon the trolley between it leaving the spring and it passing through the first light gate.

Calculate the energy in the spring's elastic potential energy store when it is compressed.

Energy = ... J

[4]

ii) Between the two light gates, a constant frictional force acts on the trolley. The distance between the two light gates is 1.00 m and the speed of the trolley at the second light gate is 0.40 m/s.

Calculate the deceleration of the trolley as it travels between the two light gates.

Deceleration = ... m/s²

[3]

c) Helene replaces the rough surface with a frictionless board. The trolley travels along the frictionless board with a speed of 0.60 m/s until it collides with a second, stationary trolley that has a mass of 0.40 kg. The first trolley stops moving and the second trolley moves off.

Calculate the velocity at which the second trolley moves after the collision.

Velocity = ... m/s

[5]

[Total 14 marks]

1 Loreen is investigating the pressures of different liquids. She fills three identical containers with a different liquid, then places a pressure sensor in each one. The sensor works by measuring the force acting on the diaphragm at its base. The sensor is held with the diaphragm at the same depth in each case, as shown in the diagram below. The table shows her results.

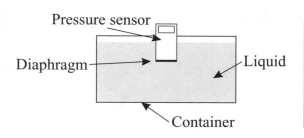

Liquid	Density (kg/m³)	Pressure detected (Pa)
Brine	1200	1800
Olive oil	800	1200
Water	1000	1500

a) Loreen measures the length and width of the diaphragm that is in contact with the different fluids.
She calculates that the pressure sensor diaphragm has an area of 5.0×10^{-3} m².
Calculate the force exerted on the diaphragm by olive oil in the experiment shown above.

Force = ... N

[4]

b) Loreen tests an unknown liquid, X. At a depth of 15 cm, the pressure caused by liquid X is 2850 Pa.
Calculate the density of liquid X. Use gravitational field strength = 10 N/kg.

Density = ... kg/m³

[4]

c) Loreen makes the following statement:

Loreen
At any depth, the pressure of liquid X is larger than the pressure of water at the same depth.

Use the particle model to explain why Loreen's statement is correct.

....

....

....

....

....

....

....

....

[4]

[Total 12 marks]

12 Zach is designing a basic electronic toy. He wants the toy to be able to light up and spin around. He creates a basic circuit of a battery connected to a motor. Zach connects two filament bulbs and a fixed resistor in parallel to the motor. The two bulbs and the resistor are all in series with each other. The bulbs and the motor can be switched on and off separately.

a) Draw the circuit diagram for the circuit created by Zach.

[5]

Zach turns on just the motor. The potential difference across the motor is 6.0 V and a current of 70.0 mA flows through the motor. After 15 minutes, he switches off the motor and measures the temperature of the motor's casing. He finds that it has increased by 6.0 °C.

The motor's casing has a mass of 25.0 g.
The material it is made from has a specific heat capacity of 120 J/kg °C.

b) Calculate the amount of energy that is usefully transferred by the motor in 15 minutes. You can assume that all the energy not transferred to the thermal energy store of the motor's casing is usefully transferred.

Energy usefully transferred = ... J

[5]

c) Explain **one** modification that Zach could make to the toy to make it more efficient.

....

....

....

[2]

[Total 12 marks]

13 The diagram on the right shows a Van de Graaff generator in which the metal dome becomes positively charged.

The Van de Graaff generator consists of a metal dome and a belt made of insulating material wrapped round two wheels. The wheels turn in order to turn the belt.

The bottom of the belt continuously brushes past metal comb A which is positively charged. The top of the belt continuously brushes past metal comb B, which is attached to the metal dome.

Grade 7-9

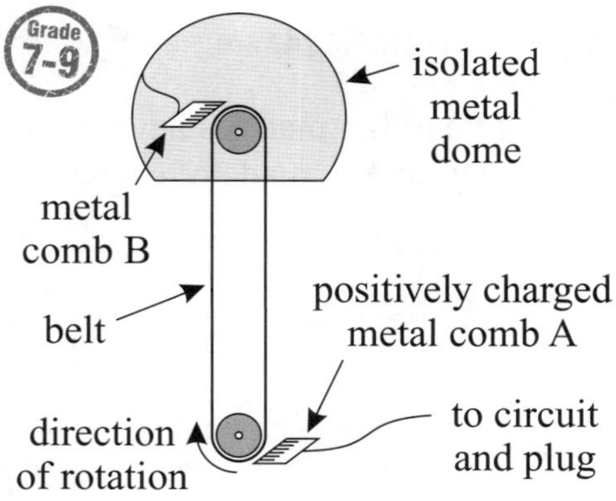

isolated metal dome

metal comb B

belt

positively charged metal comb A

direction of rotation

to circuit and plug

a) Describe how a charge builds up on the dome.

....

....

....

....

....

[4]

b) i) An earthed piece of metal is brought near the sphere. A spark is created between the dome and the piece of metal. Describe this behaviour in terms of the movement of electrons.

....

[1]

ii) Just before the spark, a charge of 15 µC has built up on the dome and the potential difference between the dome and the earthed metal is 320 kV. Calculate the energy transferred by the spark.

Energy transferred = ... J

[4]

The Van de Graaff generator is turned off after the spark. The dome has no static charge on it. Small pieces of paper confetti are placed in a pile on top of the dome. Paper is an electrical insulator. When the Van de Graaff generator is turned on, the pieces of confetti fly off the dome in different directions.

c) Explain this behaviour in terms of the charges and forces on the pieces of confetti and the dome.

....

....

....

....

....

[3]

[Total 12 marks]

Mixed Questions

14 Christine is playing with some marbles in the lab.

Two of her marbles have the same volume (4.2 cm³), but are made of different materials.
Marble A is made of rubber. She isn't sure what marble B is made of.

She finds the following table in a textbook.

Material	Average density (g/cm³)
Porcelain	2.30
Glass	2.71
Rubber	1.21
Diamond	3.53

a) Calculate the mass of marble A, using the information Christine found in the textbook.
Give your answer to **two** significant figures.

Mass of marble A = ... g
[4]

Christine balances the two marbles on a plank that is pivoted at its centre, as shown below.
The plank is level, so the clockwise and anticlockwise moments acting on the plank are equal.

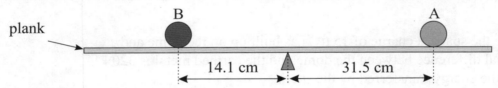

b) i) Christine determines from the experiment above that the mass of Marble B is 11.4 g,
to three significant figures. Show that Christine is correct.
Use gravitational field strength = 10 N/kg.

[5]

ii) Use your answer to part i) to determine which of the four materials listed in the table above
marble B is made from.

Material of marble B = ...
[3]

[Total 12 marks]